Looking Back

ST. CATHARINES
OUR BUILT HERITAGE

Looking Back

ST. CATHARINES
OUR BUILT HERITAGE

Erin Julian Alicia Kirk Arden Phair
St. Catharines Museum

Looking Back Press

Copyright ©2005 by St. Catharines Museum. All rights reserved. No part of this book may be reproduced, stored in a retrieval system, or transmitted in any form without written permission of the publisher.

Vanwell Publishing acknowledges the financial support of the Government of Canada through the Book Publishing Industry Development Program for our publishing activities.

Published by Looking Back Press
An Imprint of Vanwell Publishing Limited
1 Northrup Crescent, P.O. Box 2131
St. Catharines, ON L2R 7S2
For all general information contact Looking Back Press at:
Telephone 905-937-3100 ext. 829
Fax 905-937-1760
E-Mail vanessa.mclean@vanwell.com

For customer service and orders:
Toll-free 1-800-661-6136

Printed in Canada
Updated November 2006
Second printing

Library and Archives Canada Cataloguing in Publication

Julian, Erin, 1985-
St. Catharines : our built heritage / Erin Julian, Alicia Kirk, Arden Phair.

(Looking back)
"St. Catharines Museum".
Includes index.
ISBN 1-55068-948-7

1. St. Catharines, Ont.—Buildings, structures, etc.
2. Historic buildings—Ontario—St. Catharines. I. Kirk, Alicia, 1983-
II. Phair, Arden   III. St. Catharines Museum   IV. Title. V. Series:
Looking back (St. Catharines, Ont.)

FC3099.S23Z57 2005   917.13'38   C2005-906801-9

For information about the contents of this book:
St. Catharines Museum
P.O. Box 3012
1932 Welland Canals Parkway
St. Catharines, Ont. L2R 7C2
905 984-8880   905 984-6910 fax
info@stcatharineslock3museum.ca

Cover Photo: Local photographer Lloyd Snider (active in St. Catharines about 1913-17) captures this expressive image of workers preparing the wooden structural supports for what is probably the "new" hospital of the St. Catharines General Hospital (later referred to as the McSloy Wing). See page 152. (StCM N 6278)

Introduction photo, page 7: St. Catharines Museum at 343 Merritt Street, *c.*1976 • Designated 1978. N 3203, *Frank Caplan photo.*

Contents

Acknowledgements 6

Introduction 7

1. Places of Worship 9

2. Transportation 25

3. Residential 37

4. Commercial/Industrial—The Downtown 59

5. Commercial/Industrial—Grantham/Homer/ 91
   Merritton/Port Dalhousie

6. Education 117

7. Public Buildings 137

Index 156

Acknowledgements

A publication of this nature involves the efforts and input of many people. Dr. John N. Jackson, author and Professor Emeritus of Applied Geography at Brock University, first presented the opportunity to the Museum to become involved in the Looking Back series. John stands out as one of our great citizens who has done much to further the study of local history. Many of his 14 publications have featured subjects associated with the area, subjects that have been further developed by more recent authors.

The quality of this book was significantly enhanced with extensive input from Dennis Gannon, Alex Ormston, John Burtniak, Norman Macdonald, Linda Kurki, Paul Hutchinson, and Bill Salton. Collectively, they possess an amazing body of knowledge – their historical and editorial suggestions were invaluable in the final presentation of the book's content. To them the Museum extends its gratitude for late night conversations, weekends sacrificed, and time spent to meet tight deadlines. Thank you *very* much!

For additional historical assistance, we are grateful to June Green and Linda Kurki in the Museum's Library / Archives. Answers to questions about nagging dates or fine points of historical accuracy were patiently sought out, time and again. Similarly, the staff of the Museum stepped in to edit, scan, design, or undertake any tasks needed to complete the book. Likewise, the facilities of the Special Collections room of the St. Catharines Public Library, and its staff, Sandra Enskat and Elizabeth Finnie, are to be applauded for constantly furthering the cause of local history. Many others were also consulted, including Walter Asbil, Muriel Baerg, Betty Baum, Jack Collard, Ted Collins, Bob Dunn, Margaret Ferguson, Greg Finn, William German, Skip Gillham, Jon Jouppien, Stan Lapinski, Paul Lewis, The Rt. Rev. Michael McKinley, Region Niagara-Gary Ateck, Mike Smith, Bill Stevens, Lois Swayze, Corlene Taylor, Ian Wolfe, Scotiabank Archives, and others.

To MP Walt Lastewka's office and the HRSDC Summer Career Placement Program, we extend our sincere appreciation for their financial support which enabled the Museum to hire summer staff (Erin Julian) to undertake the writing and layout of the book. Thanks also to Westminster College in Pennsylvania for its co-operative education internship program which enabled Alicia Heinle-Kirk to conduct research for the project.

And lastly we would like to thank Vanessa McLean and Ben Kooter for involving the St. Catharines Museum in such a project. They are genuinely passionate about preserving and promoting the history which surrounds us. Congratulations to Vanessa, Ben, and Vanwell Publishing on making our shared heritage widely available through publications such as those in the Looking Back series.

We are pleased to present this revised edition which includes amendments and updates to about three dozen of the articles.

Arden Phair
Curator of Collections
St. Catharines Museum
October 2006

Introduction

The St. Catharines Museum is pleased to present almost 200 images from its photographic archives for this special look back at the built heritage of St. Catharines. While it is impossible to fully document the rich history of our community in such a modest-sized book, an attempt has been made to be representative of its geographic, religious, cultural, social, educational, industrial, and economic background (where images were available). And, as the home of the largest public archives for St. Catharines, the Museum would be most interested in other images (or artifacts) which residents possess which would enhance the collection and be available to share with future generations. These archival images could also become the subject matter for future photo histories by the Museum.

The St. Catharines Museum has been collecting and preserving community history since its founding in 1965. The Museum was established through the efforts of the St. Catharines & Lincoln Historical Society, the St. Catharines Jaycees, and the City of St. Catharines. The nucleus of the collection was provided by the Society (now named the Historical Society of St. Catharines). They had been collecting objects of local interest since their formation as the Lincoln Historical Society on January 21, 1927. Repositories were only temporary and this meant that the collections were displayed, stored, and moved amongst the old fire hall, the Public Library, and Rodman Hall. The Society's dream of a permanent museum came to fruition in Canada's Centennial year when the St. Catharines Historical Museum opened on June 4, 1967 in the former Merritton Town Hall. Its first director was John Smith, a former Mayor and Member of Parliament. The Museum initially occupied the ground floor, and then expanded to the second floor (and a partial third floor constructed for artifact holdings).

The need for expanded facilities that would meet modern museum standards necessitated the move to Lock 3. Since the Museum officially opened in its new quarters in 1991, it has been enjoyed by hundreds of thousands of visitors.

This publication is released on the 40th anniversary of the establishment of the St. Catharines Museum
1965-2005

We salute those community volunteers who have guided the Museum since 1965 through their participation on the Board, and in particular, those Trustees who have served as Chairs and Chairmen of the institution:

1965-69	Gordon C. Merritt	1981-83,'93	John Burtniak	1996-97	Jim Davey
1970-71	Betty Baum	1984	Colin Duquemin	1997-99	Palmier Stevenson-Young
1972	Dave Lewis	1985	Wes Turner		
1973-74	John Martin	1986	Rob Welch	2000-01	Peter Secord
1975-77	Frank Caplan	1987-91	Bill Wiley	2002, '06	David Sloan
1978-79	Norman Macdonald	1992-93	Walt Lastewka	2003-05	Ruth McMullan
1980	Phyllis Dean	1994-96	Judy Dohnberg		

Guide to Abbreviations

'	foot
"	inch
bet.	between
c.	circa (i.e. 'about')
cm	centimetre
cor.	corner
e.s.	east side
lbs.	pounds
m	metre
n.	north
n.e.	northeast
n.s.	north side
nr.	near
opp.	opposite
s.f.	square foot
s.	south
s.s.	south side
w.	west
w.s.	west side
DSBN	District School Board of Niagara
LCBE	Lincoln County Board of Education
NF	Niagara Falls
NOTL	Niagara-on-the-Lake
StC	St. Catharines
StCM	St. Catharines Museum

Terminology about the buildings reflects the name in use at the time of the photo, e.g. "Methodist" (instead of the presently used "United").

The date or approximate date of the photographs used follows the title of the article on each page, e.g. "Mary, Star of the Sea R.C. Church, c.1907"

"The Grimsby Formation" is the proper Canadian geologic name for the mottled reddish/grenish stone formation commonly referred to as either red or pink "Grimsby granite" or "Grimsby sandstone," or as "red Queenston limestone."

One
Places of Worship

MARY, STAR OF THE SEA R.C. CHURCH, *c*.1907
34 Elgin St. • Built: 1871/1993-94 • Architect: F.T. Walton (NF,NY) (1871)/Venerino P.P. Panici (StC)/Michael Mirynech (StC) (1994) • Builder: F.T. Walton (NF,NY) (1871/T.R. Hinan Contractors (StC) (1994)

The third congregation to be established in Port Dalhousie was originally named Our Lady of the Lake Roman Catholic Church. It is now known as Mary, Star of the Sea Roman Catholic Church. A popular legend tells how endangered sailors, praying to the Virgin Mary, vowed to construct a church in her name if they arrived safely in harbour. The current building resulted in 1871. The 12.2 m (40') spire, originally surmounted by a gilt cross (now an illuminated cross), can be seen from the middle of the lake, and is still used as a beacon to guide local sailors. The church itself was built of Kingston stone, with Gothic-style nave windows and a chancel window depicting the Crucifixion. During renovations and an addition in 1993-94, old records were found in a cornerstone which included details of parishioners and clergy from 1871.

BME CHURCH AND CONGREGATION, 1920s
92 Geneva St. • Built: 1855 • Designated: 1980 (exterior), 1990 (interior) /2002

Upper Canada's anti-slavery legislation of 1793 encouraged many enslaved Blacks in the United States to seek safe refuge in the British colony across the border. The last stop for many on the Underground Railroad was St. Catharines, some of whom were led by the Black Moses, Harriet Tubman. As the Black community grew, so too did their need for a church. In 1840, William Hamilton Merritt and Oliver Phelps provided a plot of land on Geneva Street for the construction of a log building, replaced in 1855 by the present British Methodist Episcopal Church (BME). In the photo, the clergy and congregation are gathered on the front steps for some special event, as noted by the ribbons on some lapels.

BME CHURCH, 1950

The British Methodist Episcopal Church (BME) was so named to distinguish it from the African Methodist Episcopal Church of the United States and to associate its members more closely with Canada and Great Britain. The Church was designed and built by its Black congregation. Whole walnut logs were used to support the floor structure and for framing, erected on a foundation of uncut stone. The exterior stucco was likely applied over wood siding in the 1920s or 1930s. The Church was protected under the Ontario Heritage Act in 1980, and was designated a National Historical Site in 2002 as a centre of Black heritage and culture.

St. Catherine of Alexandria R.C. Church, c. 1910
69 Church St. (renamed in 1855 from Academy St.) • Built: 1843-45 / 1859 / 1870

Irish Catholics came to St. Catharines to help build the Welland Canals, and stayed to build a place of worship. Their first church, St. John's, was erected on land purchased in 1832, later the site of the present church. Unfortunately, the structure was destroyed by arson on August 23, 1841. It was replaced with a 12.2 m x 24.4 m (40' x 80') stone structure renamed and dedicated to St. Catherine of Alexandria. It would be enlarged several times, the first in 1859 with the addition of a transept on the east (Church Street) side, and the second with a transept to the west, thereby completing the cruciform shape of the church. The Very Rev. W.R. Harris (Dean from 1884 through 1901), removed the original castellated tower to permit the extension of the building southwards, and was also likely responsible for the soaring interior ceiling vaults seen here. The vaults have no structural role but are altogether decorative. The stained glass in the church is particularly striking, and is believed to have been imported from Munich, Germany. The Church was elevated in status on November 25, 1958. It became the Cathedral of St. Catherine of Alexandria with the installation of the Most Rev. Thomas J. Fulton as the first Bishop of the new Diocese of St. Catharines.

St. George's Anglican Church, *c.*1905

83 Church St. • Built: 1835-40/1845/1864/1951 • Architect: Samuel Haight (StC) (original church and belfry) / John Howard (Toronto) (existing tower); Nicholson/Macbeth & successors (Parish Hall) • Builder: James Gilleland and Godfrey Waud (StC) (stonemasonry); Samuel Haight (StC) (1840) (woodwork); Samuel G. Dolson (StC) (1864) (wing)

St. George's Anglican Church has the oldest congregation in St. Catharines. The original church was founded in 1796 and a building erected thereafter near the corner of St. Paul and McGuire (formerly Yates) Streets. Known simply as the Church at St. Catharines, it was destroyed by fire in 1836, a year after work had started on the present building on Church Street. A new cemetery was opened behind the new premises. Some of the tombstones of early residents are still visible today. Subsequent additions and alterations have transformed the original rectangular shape into a more traditional cruciform. A Parish Hall and vestry additions have further concealed the original footprint. The Church is built in the Gothic Revival style, particularly evident in the windows and spire.

ST. THOMAS' ANGLICAN CHURCH, c.1910
99 Ontario St. • Built: 1877-79 • Architect: M.C. Beebe (Buffalo) • Builder: Timothy Sullivan (StC) • Designated: 1978, de-designated 1995

By the mid 1870s the Anglican population in west St. Catharines had outgrown Christ Church, and the new parish of St. Thomas was opened in 1879. Architect M.C. Beebe, a disciple of R.R. Richardson of Boston, designed the building in the Richardson Romanesque style. Located at the end of Church Street, the structure dominates the streetscape with its colourful Grimsby formation stone and its lovely rose window. A Parish Hall designed by Nicholson and Macbeth Architects was added in the 1920s. A columbarium was installed in the basement in 1983, the three decaying bartizans, removed in 1975, were replaced in 1985, and the decorative lantern at the apex of the building was restored. Five years later, Dr. Gerald Robinson, a Toronto architect, created a glass enclosed entrance with a raised circular driveway and an exterior staircase to the street for greater access. Inside, the fixed lighting was replaced with moveable theatrical lights and stationary pews were replaced with cathedral-type chairs to facilitate greater variety in worship and seating configurations.

KNOX PRESBYTERIAN CHURCH, *c*.1905
53 Church St. • Built: 1859-60

In 1859, the "Scotch Church" on Centre Street purchased land on Church Street from Orson Phelps and Henry Mittleberger to build a new Presbyterian church. The new brick church opened on May 20, 1860, with Rev. R.F. Burns as Pastor. It was renamed Knox Presbyterian Church by a congregational vote in 1875. The building is Romanesque in design with three bay windows ending in Tudor arches on the front façade. The only pictorial stained glass appears in the nave. The interior was completely renovated in 1900 when the galleries were removed, cathedral glass installed, and the pews replaced. Further improvements were made in 1919 when a new organ replaced the old, in 1928 when new lighting, a side entrance, and a memorial window for Capt. James Norris were installed, and in 1957 with the addition of the Christian Education Centre adjacent to the Church, designed by Macbeth and Williams Architects.

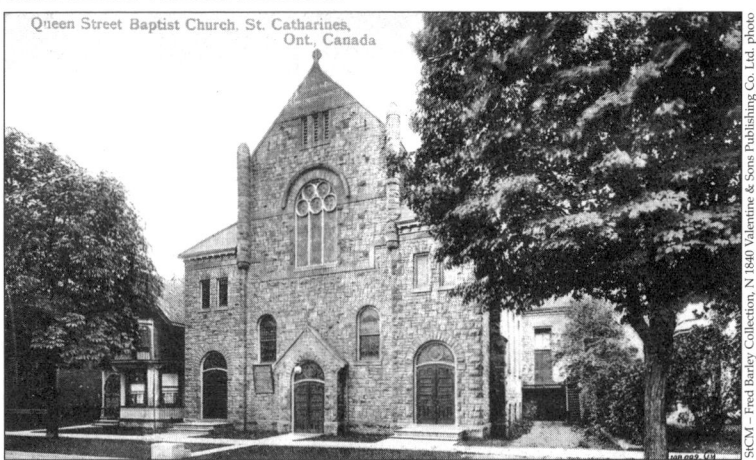

QUEEN STREET BAPTIST CHURCH, *c*.1908
57 Queen St. • Built: 1891

The Baptist congregation now located on Queen Street began in 1833, known as the Grantham Baptist Church. They were organized at the Ten Mile Creek School in Grantham Township. In 1842, the 22-member congregation moved to St. Catharines, renamed itself the First Baptist Church, and used the facilities of the Grantham Academy on Church Street. The congregation remained there, under the ministry of Dr. George Wilson, until a small wooden church was erected on Queen Street in 1844. The new Queen Street Baptist Church replaced it in 1852 at the same location, but was unfortunately ravaged by fire in 1891, leaving only the stone walls standing. The congregation and community raised money for the new stone church illustrated, built on the old site. In 1924, the stables at the rear of the church were demolished to make way for a Christian Education wing.

St. Paul Street Methodist Church, c.1905

366 St. Paul St. • Built: 1845/1875 • Builder: Henry Burgoyne (StC) (1845) / Samuel G. Dolson (StC) (1875 spire) • Designated: 1990

The first meetings of Methodists in St. Catharines were held in the home of Rufus Wright. In 1823, the congregation's original frame church opened on St. Paul Street, known as the Wesleyan Methodist Church. Henry Burgoyne was contracted in 1845 to enlarge and rebuild the church in brick. The new church, designed in Italianate and Old English Gothic style, was inspired by Grace Methodist Church in Buffalo. An impressive spire was added in 1875. An 1876 fire gutted the building, but it was rebuilt to the same design. Like all other Canadian Methodist congregations, St. Paul Street joined the United Church of Canada on its formation in 1925. The church portion was again gutted by fire on January 22, 1962, leaving only the walls and tower standing. Rebuilding eventually matched the original appearance.

Welland Avenue Methodist Church, c.1905

5 Henry St. (cor. of Welland Ave.) • Built: 1877 • Architect: Sidney Rose Badgley (StC)

The construction of the Third Welland Canal in the 1870s and 1880s attracted many workers and their families to St. Catharines. As the population grew, several new churches were established, including the Welland Avenue Methodist (now United) Church on Henry Street. The original frame church was built in 1871 and became the Sunday School after 1877 when the present brick church was built in front of it, facing onto Welland Avenue. The architect, Sidney Rose Badgley (designer of the local Oille Fountain and Toronto's Massey Hall), designed the church spire to replicate that of Magdalen College in Oxford, England. Other important architectural features include the twelve spires of the tower, representing the twelve Apostles, and the Notman Memorial Window, installed in 1913.

ST. BARNABAS ANGLICAN CHURCH, c.1910
31 Queenston St. • Built: 1893 • Architect: Charles J. Graham (Toronto) • Builder: George Wilson (StC)

St. Barnabas Anglican began in 1870 as a Mission of St. George's Anglican Church, meetings being held in Collier's Hall at the corner of Niagara and Queenston Streets. In 1873, a small wooden church, St. Barnabas Mission Chapel, was erected on Tasker Street (then called John Street). In 1891, the church building was moved to the corner of Queenston and Calvin Streets. The Grimsby formation stone for the present church, was laid on June 13, 1893, and the first service was held on September 28. The design of the Gothic Revival church was influenced by the Arts and Crafts Movement, which attempted to revive the craftsmanship and ambiance of earlier Medieval styles. The interior embodies massive timber roof construction, French-style oil-finished woodwork, Germanic and Italian windows, and ochre walls with murals recently painted by local artist Chris Tinkler. The original wooden church was used as a Parish Hall until 1935 when it was demolished.

ST. MARY OF THE ASSUMPTION R.C. CHURCH, c.1904
169 St. Paul Cres. • Built: 1875 (relocated)

The original St. Mary's Church, seen here, was named after St. Mary of the Assumption. The "T" shaped wood frame building was described as having a "striking belfry." When the present church replaced it, the old one was divided into two – one part moved to Pelham Road opposite Kent Street, and the other moved to behind St. Paul Street W. Opened for worship on February 8, 1914, the new building was one of the last buildings constructed using the increasingly scarce Grimsby formation stone.

RIDLEY MEMORIAL CHAPEL, 1923
2 Ridley Rd. • Built: 1923 • Architect: Sproat and Rolph (Toronto)

Prior to the opening of the Ridley Chapel in 1923, students from Ridley College attended services at St. Thomas' Anglican Church on Ontario Street. The Chapel, built in the Perpendicular Gothic style with stone from Georgetown, was awarded a gold medal in design from the American Institute of Architects. The Memorial Chapel honours the memory of the 61 former Ridley students who died during the First World War. Their names are inscribed on the west altar.

RIDLEY MEMORIAL CHAPEL, 1923

The interior of the Memorial Chapel contains 18 stained glass windows whose frames are made, like the Chapel doorways, from Bedford stone. The ceiling is finished with British Columbia cedar, and the chapel furniture is made of oak. A north aisle and related new pews were added in 1964. The interior also contains 66 pews. Although it began as an Anglican institution, its services today are ecumenical in nature. Many Ridley graduates continue to return to the Chapel for marriages, baptisms, and funerals.

St. Gregory the Illuminator Armenian Apostolic Church, c.1970
49 Carlton St. • Built: 1930/1995-98 • Architect: (Toronto) (1998)

When St. Gregory's opened in 1930, it was the first Armenian Church in Canada. In 1930, the Armenian community in St. Catharines numbered approximately 95 families. Levan Babayan founded the Armenian Mission of St. Catharines. The Armenian-language services upheld the traditions and customs of their faith. More than a church, the building also served as a school and community centre. Plans for an expansion were started in 1995, but unfortunately, arsonists gutted the interior of the church in 1997. The parishioners quickly rebuilt, and the following year, during celebrations of the centennial of the Armenian Church in North America, His Eminence, Archbishop Hovnan Derderian, visited the newly expanded church and consecrated 16 crosses. St. Gregory's was also honoured with their first visit from the Patriarch of the Church, His Holiness, Karekin II on May 21, 2001. The visit coincided with the 1700th anniversary of the proclamation of Christianity in Armenia.

First United Church, c. 1875
93 Church St. (renamed in 1855 from Academy St.) • Built: 1834 (demolished 1876) • Designated: 1991

Presbyterian Church services were first held in St. Catharines in 1831 at Oliver Phelps' mill at the foot of Geneva Street. As the town grew, and there were more Presbyterians, improved facilities were required. As a result, this red-brick meeting house was erected on Church Street at a cost of $4,000. It opened on October 23, 1834 with 108 worshippers celebrating the inaugural service. Rev. A.K. Buell of Cayuga, NY was the minister. The two-storey building featured a spire with eight pinnacles. Encircling the Church is a picket fence that helped to keep out stray animals. The church was demolished in 1876 to make way for the present First United Church, opened in 1878. Due to a dwindling congregation, they chose to close the handsome Church Street edifice. The final regular service at First United Church took place on February 29, 2004, after which the congregation amalgamated with Grantham United Church to form First Grantham United Church.

St. James Anglican Church, c.1910
405 Merritt St. • Builder: Newman Bros. (StC)

Merritton Anglicans initially worshipped in local homes, a railway freight shed, the village school, and the Orange Hall. In 1869, a vacant church from Port Dalhousie (St. John's Anglican), was partially dismantled, towed up the Second Canal and reassembled in Merritton. It served its new community from 1871 until it was destroyed by fire in 1892. The cornerstone was laid in June 1892 for a new brick church on the same site. In 1898, the Merritton Tornado damaged part of the steeple. A Parish Hall was added in the 1960s. The Rev. H.L.A. Almon was Rector from 1910 until 1931.

Elm Street Methodist Church and Manse, c.1911
11 Elm St. • Built: 1888/1954 (Church); 1911 (Manse) • Builder: Newman Bros. (StC) (1888)

The original congregation of the Elm Street Church was formed in 1858 and met in a private residence on Moffat Street that they called "Glory Hill." In 1888, the congregation joined with the Pine Street Wesleyan Church and shortly afterwards a new church was built on Elm Street. Officially opened January 13, 1889, it was a frame church which twenty years later was sheathed in brick veneer. Construction of the adjacent Manse commenced in 1911. The congregation voted to become a part of the United Church of Canada when it was formed in 1925. In 1954, the Elm Street United Christian Education Centre was added to the building.

St. Andrew's Presbyterian Church, c.1912-13
92 Main St. • Built: 1894

Until 1852, the small Presbyterian community in Port Dalhousie worshipped in one of the St. Catharines churches. When the community reached 32 members, however, missionary Angus McIntosh was sent by the Church of Scotland to hold separate meetings in the Port Dalhousie schoolhouse on Main Street, near the Anglican cemetery. Though not officially organized until 1852, they had already begun construction of a church in 1849, making them the second Church in Port Dalhousie. In 1894, the illustrated Church and Sunday School were constructed at a total cost of $4,500. The building looks much the same, minus the decorative bargeboard at the roofline. In June 1925 St. Andrew's joined the United Church of Canada and was renamed St. Andrew's United Church.

St. John's Anglican Church – Parish Hall, 1912
80 Main St. (cor. of Ann) • Built: 1912

The Parish of St. John's is the oldest in Port Dalhousie. It was founded in 1834 as St. James Louth and services were held in a local schoolhouse. Their first church was built in the early 1840s adjacent to the Main Street burying ground. The present St. John's Church was constructed by Samuel G. Dolson and was dedicated on June 24, 1868. At one time, the Church owned all of the land on the north side of Main Street from Ann to Elgin Street. The Parish Hall, shown here, was built on a portion of this block with the main entrance facing Ann Street. It has since been bricked in, a new vestibule entrance added to the left, and a larger addition made to the right. The Hall was renovated in 1953. In 2004 a new Parish Centre was built during the Church's 170th anniversary celebrations. The central main entrance of the old Hall has been bricked in and a new vestibule entrance added to the left.

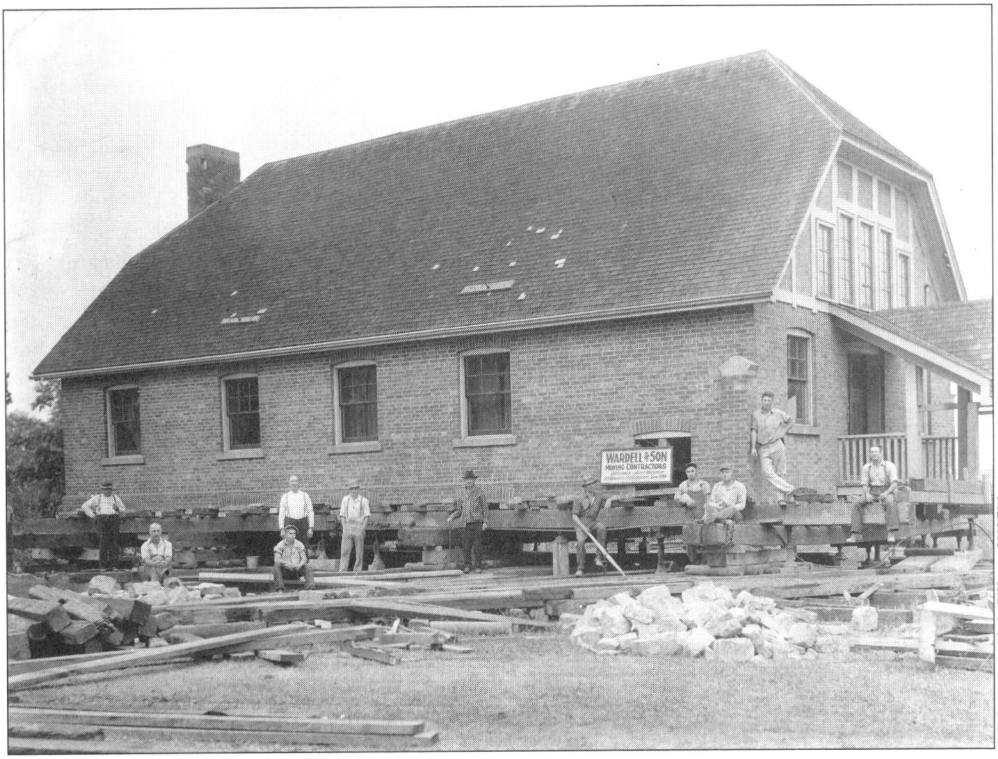

StCM – courtesy Marie O'Hearn, 2003.71.1

Christ Church (McNab) – Parish Hall, 1934

1296 McNab Rd. (McNab) • Built: 1913

The location of the Parish Hall of Christ Church (McNab) on consecrated ground had always been a bone of contention. In 1934, the Bishop took matters into his own hands and ordered the building moved. The brick behemoth was pivoted 90° counter-clockwise so that the door then faced McNab Road (before that, the door faced south, providing convenient access to the Church). Wardell and Son Moving Contractors of St. Catharines accomplished the difficult task at a cost of $2030. The company had been in the moving business since the mid-1870s. Charles E. Wardell took over Solomon and Isaac Wardell's business about 1908 and was joined by his son, Elmer, in 1929. Ads for the Queenston Street company boasted that they were a "Mover of stone, brick, and frame buildings; also raising and lowering frames and smoke stacks". Their moving operations ceased in 1964.

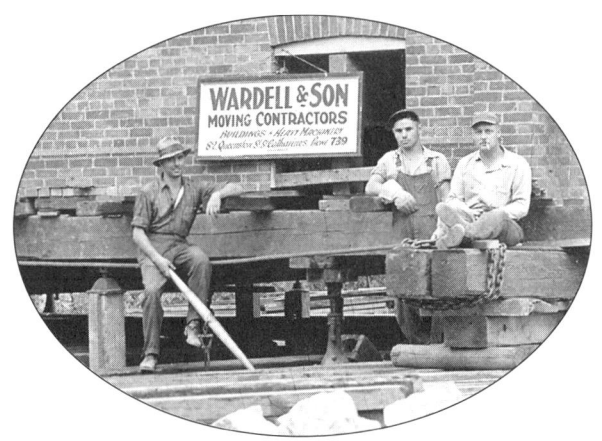

Sts. Cyril & Methodius Ukrainian Catholic Church, 1947

14 Rolls Ave. • Built: 1944-49 • Architect: Rev. Philip Ruh (Manitoba) • Designated: 1998

The first Ukrainian settlers came to St. Catharines between 1912 and 1914, and within thirty years had built this Byzantine Revival Church. The Church was named after two Thessalonian monks. Ukrainian Catholics follow the Julian Calendar rather than the Gregorian Calendar, and have celebrated the birth of Christ on January 7th since the 1500s. The Church dominates the highway-side landscape and is built over the channel of the Third Canal, which in 1934 was filled in. The Church is in the shape of a cross, facing east in the Byzantine tradition. Bishop Isidore Borecky consecrated the completed church on January 1, 1950. Inside, breathtaking iconographies by Igor Suhacev depict the teachings contained in the Bible.

MASJID AN-NOOR Mosque, 1995

117 Geneva St. • Renovated: 1993-4 by Roma Construction • Architect: Grant Sauder (Thorold)

The name of the MASJID an-NOOR Mosque means "Mosque of Light." The Mosque was built by Hussein A. Hamdani and family for Niagara's Muslim community. It is also home to the Islamic Society of St. Catharines. The present use was painstakingly adapted from its origins as an automotive dealership and tire repair facility. The Mosque opened on January 1, 1994 in the Name of Allah and in the memory of Mohammed H. Hamdani. An addition was made in 1999.

Two
Transportation

GREAT WESTERN RAILWAY STATION (MERRITTON), *c*.1884
s.s. Wedsworth St. (formerly Beech) • Built: 1880 (demolished 1937) • Architect: Joseph Hobson, GTR Engineers Office

This handsome two-storey station reflected the prestige of being on the heavily travelled line between major centres in Canada and points in the United States. Ladies in their finest and rail employees in their working gear pose for the photographer along with children hanging out the station's open window. Steam engine #802 of the Grand Trunk Railway (formerly a GWR engine) stands at the ready. The Great Western Railway station in Merritton provided rail service for both through and local passenger and freight trains. The second storey served as the living quarters for the Stationmaster and his family, and, after he built his own home on Oakdale Avenue, the Telegraph Operator occupied it. A Freight Shed was located west of the station, while across the street was the Railway Hotel, later occupied by railway workers and nowadays a private residence at 14 Wedsworth Street. The station was razed in 1937 because it was no longer needed. A new station had been built by the GTR in 1897 that was 400 metres (1.25 miles) distant, on the north side of the tracks east of Merritt Street. It too is gone, destroyed by fire in October 1994.

Grand Trunk Railway Station (St. Catharines), c.1917
5 Great Western St. • Built: 1898 • (demolished c.1917-18)

In 1853, the Great Western Railway (GWR) provided the first rail service to St. Catharines. It ran on approximately the current east-west line from Hamilton through to Niagara Falls. Unfortunately, the rail line's location in St. Catharines was not convenient to the community, being well west of the town in an area that became known as "Western Hill". The Grand Trunk Railway (GTR) acquired the GWR in 1882. This wood-frame station was built in 1898 and was the second to occupy the site. In this winter scene, a throng of citizens and soldiers spills over onto the tracks. In 1917-18, this structure was replaced by the present enlarged and modernized brick station, one of the last built by the GTR as Canadian National Railways acquired it in 1923.

NS&T Station (Merritton), *c.*1910
n.s. of Merritt St. (w. of Bessey) • (demolished 1938)

With seating for 52, streetcar #54 is shown northbound at the Merritton Station. It is about to cross the Thorold-Merritton local line, also referred to as the "Low Line." The car is on the Main Line of the NS&T, called the "High Line" because of its elevated tracks. Open-sided streetcars, like #54, were banned in 1915. This streetcar, and other similar ones, was rebuilt in 1916 by the Preston Car & Coach Co. (Cambridge) as a centre-aisle, end-loading car with wire-mesh sides. Car 54, which was built in 1900 by the Crossen Car Mfg. Co. of Cobourg, was scrapped in 1933. The Low Line through Merritton ceased operations on May 31, 1931 and the station was demolished seven years later.

NS&T Station (St. Catharines), *c.*1905
164 St. Paul St. • (demolished *c.*1929-30)

The NS&T (Niagara, St. Catharines, and Toronto) Railway had its beginnings in 1879 as the horse-drawn St. Catharines Street Railway. The system was electrified in 1887, and lines eventually extended to Thorold, Niagara Falls, Fonthill, Welland, Port Colborne, and Niagara-on-the-Lake. This station on St. Paul Street served from 1901 until 1924 when a new terminal was opened at the corner of Geneva Street and Welland Avenue to bypass the increasing congestion of the downtown. The terminal was temporarily used by Roger Miller & Sons contractors in 1926 and as the Terminal Garage in 1929, after which it was demolished.

NS&T/CNR STATION (ST. CATHARINES), c.1930
116-124 Geneva St. • Built: 1924 (demolished 1988)

The main terminal of the CNR's NS&T division was built of brick and imported Tyndall limestone at a cost of $100,000. The upper floor of the two-storey building held the NS&T's general offices, while the ground floor contained ticket offices and waiting areas. The station had six "roofed" platforms, with Lakeshore Road and Welland Avenue cars departing from Platforms #1 and #2, Main Line cars departing from Platforms #3 and #4, and Grantham Division cars departing from Platforms #5 and #6. In 1925, buses were introduced, with regular bus service commencing in 1929. Use of the NS&T peaked in 1948 at 14.67 million passengers. The post-War popularity of the automobile and other transportation alternatives led to the rapid decline of the NS&T. By 1954 the Geneva Street station had rented out its waiting area to a local bank, and in 1955 the NS&T offices moved into Welland Avenue car barns at the site of the current Midtown Plaza. The last run of the NS&T was in 1959 when a streetcar went from Thorold to Port Colborne. The old streetcar terminal was demolished in June 1988 and replaced with the Geneva Square plaza.

AIRPORT INN, 1938
Highway 8 (s.s., e. of Coon Rd., NOTL)

In 1928, Fred Pattison and Jack Haney of Haney Auto Service, and City Solicitor Murton Seymour, purchased the Miller-Pringle property on Highway 8 east of Homer for a community flying club to train civilian pilots. The Haney Auto Service opened a gas station and took over the operation of what was to become the Airport Inn. It was located on Highway 8 at the approach to the Airport (now Coon Road). The Inn included both a dining room and a dance hall, plus served as a bus stop for inter-city travellers and area residents. The Depression made things difficult for the Flying Club and, about 1936, it was necessary to relocate it to 26.7 hectares (66 acres) on Niagara Stone Road rented from the Welstead family, the current location of the Niagara District Airport. The Airport Inn was further bypassed in 1939 when the QEW replaced Old Highway 8 as the main cross-Peninsula highway. The Dingles and Pagets continued to operate the Inn for a while, however, it is believed its last dance was on the evening of the great New Year's Eve storm of December 31, 1948.

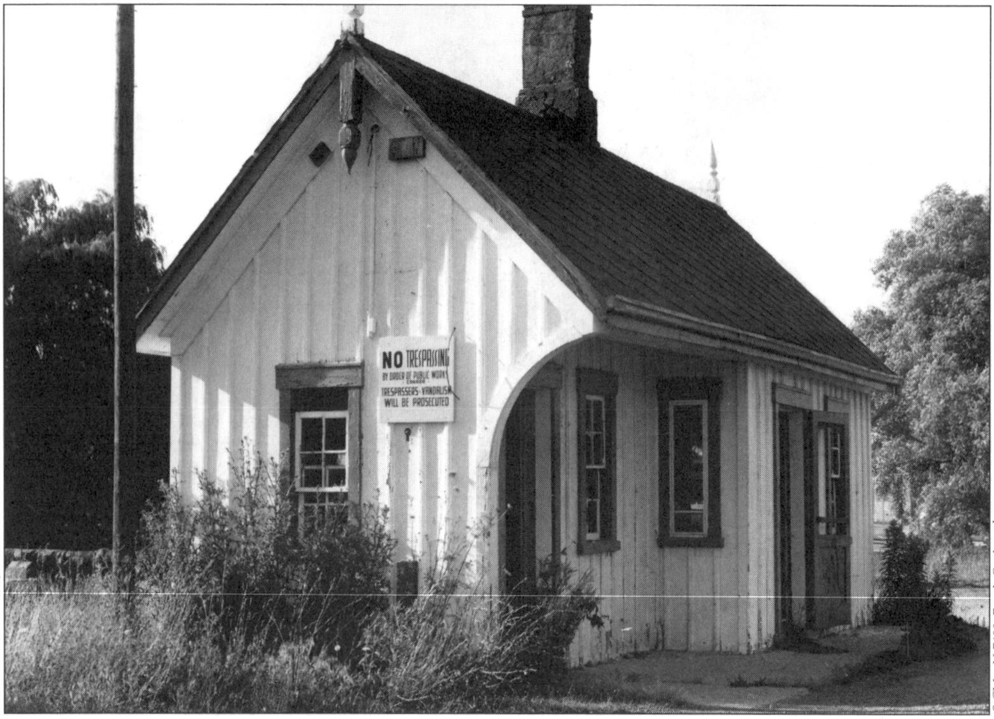

StCM – N 7490 Frank Caplan photo

LOCKTENDERS' SHANTY, *c.*1977

50 Lakeport Road, Lock 1, Third Welland Canal (n. of Lakeport Rd.) • Built: *c.*1883 • Designated: 1995, de-designated 2003

Now owned by the City of St. Catharines, the Government of Canada originally owned this Locktenders' Shanty in Port Dalhousie. The Locktender collected fees, recorded information and assisted in the locking through of passing ships. Some of the Locktenders who worked in this 3.7 m x 5.5 m (12′ x 18′) building included: John Woodall Sr., John Woodall Jr., Richard Hutton, Henry McAvoy Sr., John Paxton, and Richard Read. This Locktenders' Shanty was used during the operation of the Third Welland Canal (1881-1931). When Locks #1-3 of the Welland Ship Canal opened on April 21, 1930, the northern entrance of the canal was moved to Port Weller. This was the last lock of the Third Canal to remain in service providing access until 1968 to the shipyard on Martindale Pond successively operated by Muirs, the Port Dalhousie Shipyards Ltd., and Port Weller Dry Docks.

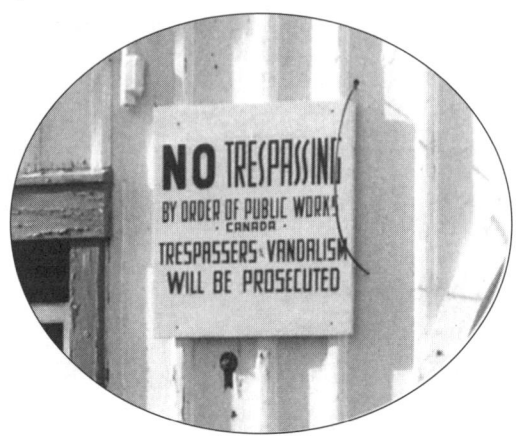

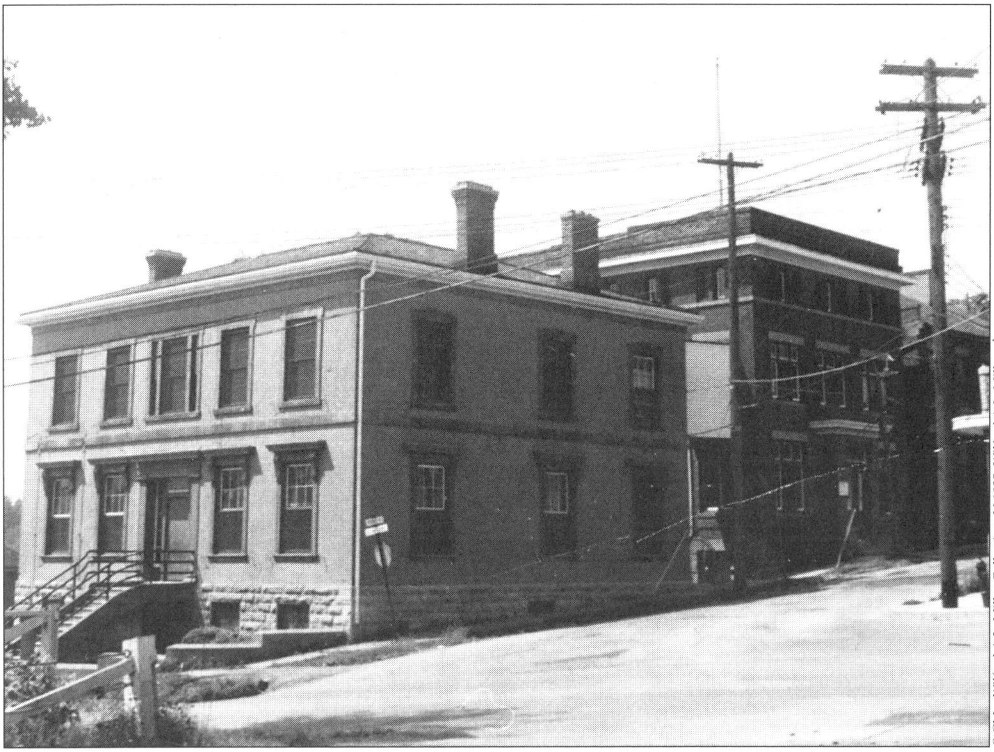

StCM – Wilfred A.L. Miller Collection, N 1035 Wilfred A.L. Miller photo

WELLAND CANAL OFFICE, *c.*1965

32 St. Paul Cres. • Built: 1855 (demolished 1970)

The Welland Canal Co. office was also used as an early Customs House (an earlier building used for the same purpose, built at the same location in 1835 was demolished and replaced in 1855). An adjacent brick building, built about 1912-14, was specifically for use as offices for Chief Engineer J.L. Weller and the construction of the Welland Ship Canal. The older building, which had been built by the Department of Public Works, was demolished in 1970 after the new Western Region offices of the St. Lawrence Seaway Authority were opened on Glendale Avenue in 1965. The former office and other adjacent buildings were removed as part of the works for Highway 406.

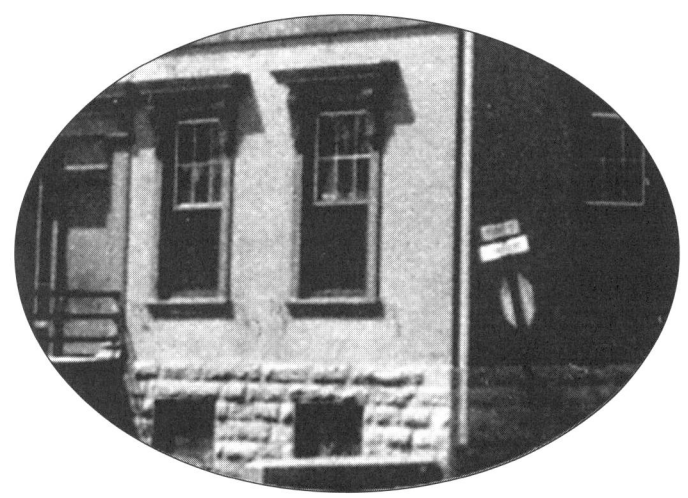

LINCOLN TRANSFORMER STATION, 1970
Lock 3, Second Canal (nr. Dittrick St.) • (demolished 1976)

When electricity came into widespread use, there also came a need for a larger and more efficient distribution system. William Cooke and Sons operated from the former Shickluna Shipyard site near Lock 3 and in 1901, their Cooke Electric Co. was purchased by the newly organized Lincoln Electric Light and Power Co. The Company supplied St. Catharines and the Welland Canal with power (the poles carrying the power lines over the Second Canal were once the tallest concrete structures in the world, owing to the need to clear the masts of passing ships). Ontario Hydro purchased the electrical distribution station from the Lincoln Electric Light and Power Company in 1933 and later transferred it to the St. Catharines Public Utilities Commission (PUC). When demolished in 1976, a crane with a wrecking ball was needed to knock down its thick concrete walls.

SHELL HOUSE – StCRC, 1977
45 Lakeport Rd. (w. of R.C.L. Branch #350) • Built: *c.*1880s (demolished 1977)

This warehouse was originally part of a complex of buildings in the Government Gate Yards at Port Dalhousie and was used for lumber storage. Its column-free design would later prove ideal for the storage of shells and oars by the St. Catharines Rowing Club. It was used as a boathouse for visiting crews as early as the 1903 Henley Regatta. In 1936, the St. Catharines Rowing Club obtained a lease for the building from the Federal Government. The oarsmen's repair shop, meeting rooms, showers, and dining rooms were on the upper level, and a dock was located across the road. The old powder blue, tin-clad Shell House remained in use until a new Shell House was built on Henley Island in 1967.

HACK FARM, 1914
Grantham Twp. (e.s. of Canal between Locks 1 and 2) • Built: pre-1900 (demolished c.1962)

Ernest H. Hack was a Grantham Township fruit farmer. Unfortunately, the farm's location was right in the path of the planned route for the Welland Ship Canal, halfway between Locks 1 and 2 near Church-Linwell Road. The property and buildings of many farmers and landowners had to be expropriated for the construction of the Canal. This meant that the Hack farm's distinctive turn-of-the-century, 8-loft barn, seen here on the channel's east bank, would have to be removed. The Hacks used the barn for both equipment and livestock. Its adjunct building even included a bell tower. The corner of the barn was sliced off at an angle for the Canal. It was later subdivided and one-half was moved to the Canal's west side, now occupied by a subdivision. The remaining east-side property was expropriated in the 1950s and the remaining half-barn, along with two nearby family homes, was demolished about 1962-63 as part of the aborted plans for an enlarged canal system featuring 'super-sized locks'. Both halves of the barn are now demolished. Bridge 3 was planned for this location but never built.

WELLAND SHIP CANAL GREENHOUSE AT PORT WELLER, *c.*1940
329A Lakeshore Rd. (w. of Lock 1, WSC) • Built: 1929 • Builder: Lord & Burnham Co. Ltd. (StC)

Decorative gardens featuring floral beds, rock gardens, and a greenhouse were built at Lock 1, a prime location viewed as a future "extension of the Niagara River Boulevard" – Lakeshore Road drive. In 1930, 150,000 bedding plants and annuals were propagated in the glass house and set out in beds. Flowers and ornamental shrubs were laid out to improve the grounds around this and other locks. The Friends of Malcolmson Park acquired the greenhouse in 1998 and undertook its restoration. The adjacent Malcolmson Park is the largest publicly owned woodlot in Niagara.

WELLAND SHIP CANAL OFFICE & STOREHOUSE – FORESTRY & MNTC. BRANCH, c.1929
believed to be located east of Lock 1 off of Broadway Avenue

Once construction of the Welland Ship Canal neared completion, the Forestry and Maintenance Branch began the task of landscaping the canal corridor, which had cut a 43.5 km (27 mile) swath across the Niagara Peninsula. Initiated in 1927, and carrying on for the next four years, the Forestry division began its work with six nurseries, an arboretum, and a seed bed. Canal banks were re-sodded to stabilize exposed ground, and trees (such as deep-rooted willows and poplars), were planted along the Canal (321,000 by 1930) to create a windbreak for ships or to prevent erosion and mudslides. While much of their work was functional, Canal leaders had visions of sanctuaries for land birds and waterfowl that would enhance the natural environment.

WELLAND SHIP CANAL ENGINEERING STAFF HOME, c.1914
location unknown

It took the talents and skills of many different engineering specialists to complete the Welland Ship Canal, including Designing, Bridge, Mechanical, Electrical, and Hydraulic Engineers. Both the Department of Railways and Canals and the Welland Ship Canal employed their own engineers, some of whom lodged in this home for engineering staff. John Laing Weller was the Engineer-in-Charge from 1912 until 1917, and Alexander Joseph Grant assumed the position from 1919 to 1932. Planning for the Fourth Welland Canal took from 1907 until 1912. Construction commenced in 1913, but was suspended from late-1916 until 1919 owing to a shortage of materials and manpower caused by the First World War. Almost 120 engineers were employed in the years leading up to the completion of the Canal in 1932.

PORT WELLER DRY DOCKS, late-1940s
located 340 Lakeshore Road East, e.s. Welland Ship Canal above Lock 1

In 1946, Charles A. Ansell, having tried unsuccessfully to buy the Muir Bros. Dry Dock in Port Dalhousie, initiated the formation of the Port Weller Dry Docks, incorporated on April 25, 1946. Ansell negotiated a lease of the dry dock and 12.9 hectares (32 acres) of Federal land. They took in their first ships on April 3rd, the *Dalhousie City* and the *Windsolite*, for their inspections. The shipyard has built, rebuilt, and repaired freighters, tankers, passenger boats, tugs, dredges, barges, naval and other vessels. Ansell eventually achieved ownership of the dry dock he had originally sought to purchase. On December 4, 1953, Port Weller Dry Docks Limited bought the former Muir Brothers site and used it for the next fifteen years for scrapping and other work on old Third Canal vessels, which could reach the dry dock via the still-operational Third Canal Lock 1. The vessel in the dry dock is believed to be a car/train ferry, either the *Ontario No. 1* or the *Ontario No. 2*. In tribute to the noted shipbuilder, the *Charles A. Ansell Gateway* is being developed opposite the dry dock in a partnership between the shipbuilder, the St. Catharines Rotary Club Lakeshore, two unions and other supporters.

Three
Residential

COOK-GILLELAND HOME (*Westchester Place*), 1890S
211 Queenston St. • Built: 1848 (demolished 1956)

In the 1840s, Moses Cook built this home at the present-day corner of Queenston Street and Eastchester (then known as Westchester). The Cook home retained its old name of "Westchester Place" long after the street was renamed. The two-storey brick home stood on 6.5 hectares (16 acres) of land, and along with Rodman Hall, was one of the first St. Catharines homes to have indoor plumbing. In 1867, the property passed to Moses' daughter, Annie, and her husband, William Gilleland (St. Catharines Mayor in 1897-98). William died in 1899. Annie and one of her sons continued to live in the house until c. 1906-11 when they moved to a fruit farm on Lakeshore Road West. The house was then occupied by Robert Peak from 1912 until 1916, was vacant in 1917, and was then remodelled by the City and County Councils for use as a Children's Shelter, c. 1917-36. After being vacant for another year, in 1937, it was then divided into apartments and used as such until 1947. From 1948 through 1983 it was a Home for the Blind known as "Linwell Hall." Westchester Place remained as a separate residence, but when room was needed for an expansion to Linwell Hall in 1956, the old home was demolished. From 1975 until 1983, the building was shared with a home for seniors. Linwell Hall has been used exclusively for the Queenchester Terrace Retirement Residence since about 1983-84.

JAMES MCSLOY HOME (*Suncroft*), c.1904
64 Church St. • Built: 1890 (demolished 1971)

James McSloy and his wife Bessie were both avid equestrians. They ran the local "Hunt Club" from their Church Street home, *Suncroft*. The three-storey brick residence was also a focal point for St. Catharines socialites. Many evening events were held at the McSloy residence, one of the first St. Catharines homes with electricity (see Hugh McSloy article). James died on April 10, 1926. Bessie died 17 years later. In 1948, the Catholic Church acquired the home for use as the Parish Centre for St. Catherine of Alexandria Church. The City purchased the building in 1971 and had it demolished in July of the same year.

HUGH MCSLOY HOME, c.1920
157 King St. • Built: 1896 (demolished 1975)

Brothers James and Hugh McSloy owned and operated the Canada Hair Cloth Company. Hugh's red-brick Italianate home was also one of the first to be lit by electricity, the electricity being generated at the family-owned Canada Hair Cloth factory and transmitted to the two adjacent McSloy residences by a private pole line on Carlisle Street (then called Chestnut). Later, the home was also equipped with an elevator. Hugh McSloy died on May 2, 1924 and his wife, Annie, occupied the house until 1951. The building was then used as offices. Thomas R. Wiley and Macdonald & Zuberec Architects were there between 1954 and 1967. It was demolished in May 1975 to provide additional parking for the Police station.

SAMUEL DE VEAUX WOODRUFF HOME (*De Veaux Hall*), c.1915
199 Ontario St. • Built: 1877 (demolished 1940)

Samuel De Veaux Woodruff, engineer and superintendent on the Welland Canal, built this redbrick residence as the central building on his large estate. It was an elegant building with a gabled metal roof, striped awnings, and tall English windows. The building passed to Welland Woodruff after the death of Samuel in 1904. When Welland in turn died in 1920, his widow continued living there until 1934. After the home was demolished, the bricks were used to build houses on Queen Mary Drive (located on a portion of the old estate). The stone stables at the rear were converted into apartments (now 36 Queen Mary Drive), while the gatehouse eventually became a medical office at 199 Ontario Street.

HAMILTON WOODRUFF HOME, c.1915
168 Ontario St. • Built: 1906-07 (demolished 2005)

While Welland Woodruff resided with his father at De Veaux Hall, the younger Woodruff son, Hamilton K. Woodruff, built his own home across from the present Hotel Dieu Hospital. Hamilton was the local Assistant Registrar and a Water Works Commissioner. He died in 1932, leaving the building to his wife, who continued living there until 1943. The building remained vacant until 1947 when the Religious Hospitallers of St. Joseph purchased it. Between 1948 and 1953 the home was used as the new Hotel Dieu maternity hospital. It was later used as a Medical Arts building comprised mostly of offices. No longer suitable for this purpose, it stood vacant for some four years and was demolished in 2005.

MERRITT HOME *(Oak Hill)*, 1900
12 Yates St. • Built: 1860 • Architect: William Thomas (Toronto)

This home was built by the Hon. William Hamilton Merritt to replace an earlier one that had been destroyed by fire in 1858. Known as "Oak Hill," the house was designed and built in the Italianate style with Neo-Classic pediments. The original roof was gabled, whereas later additions to the rear of the building are flat-roofed. The first-floor windows were decorated with pediments and decorative brackets, and the front entrance had six-panelled double doors and a stately portico. A decorative cast-iron fence on a stone base enclosed the property. The house was sold in 1933 as part of the Emily Alexandrina Merritt estate and converted into an inn. In 1938, E.T. Sandell purchased the building for use as the permanent home of St. Catharines' first radio station, CKTB.

FORMER MERRITT CARRIAGE HOUSE, *c.*1968
12A Yates Street (behind CKTB)

In 1933, E.T. Sandell established a radio station (CKTB) in the Welland House Hotel. Its tower was Canada's first vertical radio antenna, and so Sandell – also owner of the Taylor and Bate Brewery – named his company the Silver Spire Broadcasting Station Ltd. He not only included the initials of his brewery in the call letters of the station (CKTB), he also named one of its beers Silver Spire. In 1938, the station moved to the Oak Hill mansion and changed its frequency to 1550 kHz, increasing service to 241 km (150 miles). After the death of Sandell, the station was bought in 1944 by Maj. Henry B. Burgoyne and turned over to his son, Bill Burgoyne. On February 1950, the station's frequency changed to 620, and became the present 610 on April 13, 1959. The station was upgraded to 5000 watts on November 11, 1961. The handsome brick carriage house of the Merritts is in behind the stately home.

SHICKLUNA HOUSES, 1962
73-73A St. Paul Cres. • Built: *c.*1835 (demolished 1977)

The original building at 73 St. Paul Crescent was built about 1835 as a single dwelling, but around 1920 was converted to a duplex. Louis Shickluna, marine architect, shipwright, ship builder and owner, bought the house in 1845. He owned a number of houses in the vicinity for use by his workers. Shickluna died in 1880 and this house was sold six years later. It is said that the pantry, kitchen, and utility room were detached and made into a small dwelling on Newton Street.

Rodman Hall, *c.*1880

109 St. Paul Cres. • Built: 1853/1856/1862-63/1961/1975 • Architect: Salter & Fleming (1961) (StC), Macdonald & Zuberec (1975) (StC)

Rodman Hall was built in stages for Thomas Rodman Merritt, third surviving son of the Hon. William Hamilton Merritt, and his wife Mary Benson, niece of Senator James Rae Benson. It was designed in the Renaissance Revival style and contained twelve fireplaces. The Merritts lived in Rodman Hall until the death of T.R. Merritt in 1906. The home then passed to their nephew, Dr. William Hamilton Merritt (grandson of the Hon. W.H. Merritt). Upon his death, Rodman Hall was inherited by his only son, also named Thomas Rodman Merritt. In 1959, Rodman Hall was purchased by the St. Catharines and District Arts Council and opened as an art gallery the following year. Wings were added to the building in 1961 and 1975. The Arts Centre was turned over to the management of Brock University in 2003.

WALKER HOME (WINTER), 1903
1 Montebello Place (renamed in 1961 from Park Place, and earlier from William St.)

James Nichol Walker graduated from the Ontario College of Pharmacy about 1900 and established a pharmacy at 28 Queen Street with business partner John Abbs. Walker left the partnership in 1913 or 1914 to open his own pharmacy at 297 St. Paul Street, which operated until his death in 1929. Walker served on St. Catharines City Council in 1904 and 1905. He was also an avid cyclist, was President of the Athletics Lacrosse Club, and was a member of the St. Catharines Lawn Bowling Club, the Temple Lodge of Masons, and First United Church.

WALKER HOME (SUMMER), *c.*1908

Robert Walker was the first Superintendent of Montebello Park. His son, James Walker, lived in this house across from the Park from about the turn-of-the-20th-century until 1911. After that, he moved next door to 5 Midland St. He is last listed there in 1926, and his widow, Lida, in 1944. V.D. Macleod, manager of the Bank of Nova Scotia, lived at 1 Montebello Place after the Walkers. The house was built in the early-1870s for Edwin S. Leavenworth, a local printer.

GREENWOOD-O'LOUGHLIN RESIDENCES, 1976
127-129 Ontario St. • Built: 1874

Caroline Mack built the semi-detached house at 127 Ontario Street and lived there until 1904. The red-brick home was built in the English style. A skylight was cut into the roof that was aligned with openings in the floors allowing light to reach the ground floor. The interior also featured a curved staircase and two marble fireplaces, one on each floor. The house passed to John Gibb in 1904 and Edward Voisard in 1917, before Dr. W.T. Greenwood purchased #127 in 1920, and Mary O'Loughlin purchased #129 in 1919. The Greenwoods lived in the building for five years, but the O'Loughlin family stayed on for fifty years. The house appears to have been vacant after the death of Kathleen O'Loughlin in 1975 and before Gordon Stewart commenced renovations in 1977. In 2005, the building was occupied by Dr. I. Lewkowitz, and by John Kazmir's interior design firm, Studio 76.

Dr. William Chapman Home, c.1930
48 Church St. / 114 James St. (James St. renumbered in 1930 from #62) • Built: c.1905 (demolished c.1973) • Architect: Thomas H. Wiley (StC)

Dr. William J. Chapman, and his wife, Gladys, built this house at 48 Church Street for about $6000. It was diagonally opposite the old Carnegie Library and though it faced Church Street (#48), the family always used 114 James Street as their address. This side entrance on James Street also provided access to Dr. Chapman's physician's practice in the basement of the spacious brick dwelling. Dr. Chapman died in 1950 and nine years later his widow, Gladys, moved to Springbank Drive. The Church Street home remained vacant until 1961 when F.A. Muller purchased it. The Muller family lived there until 1970 at which time the building was occupied by Dr. B.M. Lennox, ophthalmologist. The building, and #50 next door, was torn down in 1972, or just after, and the Taro office complex was built in its place about 1973.

The Waud–Norris Home, *c.*1860
9 Norris Pl. (formerly Ann St., cor. of Cherry) • Built: *c.*1850 • Designated 1980; De-designated 1995; Distinct Designation August 11, 1996

The home on the corner of Ann (renamed Norris after the City's amalgamation with surrounding areas in 1961) and Cherry Streets was originally built for Godfrey Waud. In 1876, Capt. James Norris, owner of various mills and ships, married into the Waud family, and the home passed into his possession. A stone coach step with the Norris name is located by the street. The decorative fence has been removed and the rear portion of the building has been replaced with an addition of smaller proportions. The building remained in the Norris family until 1977, when Rev. Hugh Rose purchased it. Years later, it was purchased by Astride and Marjorie Tacinelli. The Norris home is now part of the Yates Street Heritage District.

HAWKEN HOME, *c.*1904-05
9 Centre St.

Posing for the camera on the small porch of their downtown home is the Hawken family, including: Edwin Hawken and his wife Mary Ann Phelps Hawken, and their two children, Robert E. Hawken and Gertrude Hawken. R.E. Hawken was an 1899 graduate of the University of Toronto and his son, James P., would marry Isabella Frampton. James and Isabella Hawken jointly operated the Dominion Electric Company. Dominion rewired used incandescent light bulbs for the Packard Electric Company, until Packard got out of the reconditioning business in 1907. Dominion, renamed The Dominion Tungsten Lamp Factory after the death of James in 1918, took over that end of the business and stayed with it until the mid-1920s. Isabella Hawken was a female pioneer in business, both as a foreman at the Packard Electric Co., and later as the owner of her own electrical company.

John J. Conlon Home, c.1910
27 Carlisle St. (formerly Chestnut) • (demolished)

John J. Conlon and his wife Margaret resided at this home from 1910 until 1918, located approximately where the Carlisle Street Parking Ramp stands today. The Conlons lived at 46 Church Street from 1923 until 1953. In addition to his work as a contractor, John Conlon also owned and managed a gravel pit at different times, and held various jobs on the Welland Canal including captain, tugmaster, and watchman.

CONLON HOME, c.1910
44-46 Church St. • (demolished c.1954-56)

Thomas Conlon (1848-1923) was a successful contractor who, with his brother John as partner, had a hand in the construction of the Welland Canal and the dredging of the Toronto harbour, as well as being a miller, landowner, and shipowner. While he was active in the affairs of Thorold, and lived there for many years, from 1910 until 1922 he resided at 44 Church Street in St. Catharines (it is believed to be Thomas who is posing for this photo). After his death in 1923, his wife, Anne, continued to live in the house until 1927. Their son, John J. Conlon then assumed ownership. He lived in the other half of the semi-detached home at 46 Church Street from 1923 until 1953. The property was purchased in 1954 for the new Federal Building (built 1956-57).

GREENWOOD HOME, c.1900
25 Church St. • Built: c.1868-69

Hiram Leavenworth's family were noted newspapermen, including publisher's of *The Farmers' Journal & Welland Canal Intelligencer*, lived at this site in a one-storey brick dwelling from 1849 until the 1850s. William Greenwood, co-owner of the Holmes and Greenwood carriage-making business, purchased the property in 1858 and built this red-brick dwelling. The house remained in the family until about 1941. Since 1990, the building has housed a variety of small businesses, including ICN, a local internet provider, whose Church Street operations began there in 1994.

MCINTYRE HOME, *c*.1890
Carlisle St. (formerly Chestnut) • (demolished)

Thomas McIntyre, who operated a cabinet making, upholstery, and undertaking business at the corner of St. Paul and Carlisle Streets, owned this canal-view home in the second half of the 19th century. The home passed to the son of Thomas and Helen McIntyre, John Brewer McIntyre, after Thomas' death. John founded the Ontario Undertakers' Association, was a member of the Independent Order of Oddfellows, and was Mayor of St. Catharines, 1889-90 and 1901-02.

DITTRICK HOME, *c.*1920
44 Westchester Ave. [W.] (renamed Westchester Ave. in 1928, then renamed again and renumbered to 116 Westchester Cres. in 1951) • (demolished *c.*1963)

Jacob Dittrick (1755-1828) was among the first to settle in St. Catharines. Settling along Twelve Mile Creek, he and his wife, Margaret Pickard, had eleven children. Their oldest son, Robert (1783-1847), married three times. The eighth child from his second marriage (to Hannah Bonnet) was Duncan (1838-1905), who married Martha Harper (1839-1924). Duncan was a prominent merchant in the coal and wood trade. Duncan and Martha Dittrick lived at 44 Westchester Avenue West. Martha is possibly shown in the photo. She continued to live at their Westchester address after the death of Duncan in 1905. It was vacant as of 1925. John L. Black and his family resided there from 1927 until the home was removed sometime after 1963 as part of the construction plans for Highway 406.

MILLER HOME, *c.*1890
379 Queenston St. • Built: 1822 (demolished)

Lewis Travers built this home. In 1882, it was sold to George Miller, a relation of Travers through marriage. After his death, the home passed to his son. When the son died in 1960, the St. Catharines Board of Education, which had expropriated the property ten years earlier, had the 138-year-old home demolished. The Miller house was located where the present-day Derby Lane meets Queenston Street. This road provides access to a cluster of houses to the north on Shetland Crescent. This is adjacent to the grounds of the old St. Catharines Riding and Driving Club and near Kernahan Park Secondary School (opened 1967).

J. Albert Pay Home, *c.*1890
Louth St. (Lock 2 Hill, Second Canal) • (demolished 1960s-70s)

The Pay brothers, John Albert (Bert) and William Henry, both had fruit farms on the west side of Twelve Mile Creek near Welland Vale. Before the re-alignment of Louth Street with Martindale Road, Albert's farm was located at what was referred to as Lock 2 Hill (today's easterly end of Ridley Heights Plaza), while William's was just north, located on Prospect Hill (now Sawmill Road). Twice married, Albert's first wife was Sarah (unknown surname) and his second wife was Kate Boyle. His first trade was as a tinsmith. In addition to farming, in the 1890s he was a partner in Titterington and Pay flour and feed. After moving off of the farm at the turn of the century, Albert was elected City Clerk for St. Catharines. Albert also served as a Councillor, Deputy Reeve and Reeve of Grantham Township, a Lincoln County Councillor, a St. Catharines Alderman, Inspector of the Lincoln County Industrial Home, Secretary of the Lincoln Agricultural Society, and was a Past Grand of the Empire Lodge #87 of the IOOF. Albert and Kate both died in 1926.

Herrick Avenue Home, c.1929
45 Herrick Ave. (cor. of Wills St.)

With street names like Clayburn and Woodburn, it isn't hard to guess what the major industry was in the Queenston Street and Westchester Avenue area in the early-1900s. The Paxton and Bray Brick Yard was literally in the backyards of many of the area's homes, homes with a common material of construction. This house was one of three identical brick homes on the north side of Herrick Avenue, west of Wills Street. And, adjacent to these homes, were four others built of brick, but to a different design. Many of the area's residents worked in the yard, part of 7.3 hectares (18 acres) rich in clay deposits. William Parnall started making bricks in that part of town in the early 1800s (he purchased the property in 1814 and built the area's first brick dwelling, sometime prior to 1832). After several other owners, Fred Paxton and Walter Bray made bricks there from 1903 until the 1950s when Sam Burnstein operated the business.

Collier Apartments, 1951
17-19 Collier St. • Built: 1951

The construction of a new apartment block was big news in St. Catharines in 1951. This photograph by Don Sinclair of *The Standard* shows 21 dignitaries gathered to mark the July 24th cornerstone laying for the "Collier Apartments." Pictured from left to right are: ?, ?, ?, Ald. Wallis, ?, ?, ?, Ald. Barley, Doug Hunter, PUC, Mayor Dick Robertson, J.E. Baston (possible), Murton Seymour, ?, ?, Bill Burgoyne, ?, Ald. John Franklin, ?, ?, ?, ?. The initials on the stone, "J.E.B.", stand for John E. Baston, a local realtor who developed the property to provide the city with "modern, convenient housing."

THOMPSON HOME, *c.*1899
Smythe St. • Built: 1898 • Builder: Richard Thompson (Merritton)

Richard Thompson built what was probably the area's first horseless steam-powered carriage in 1897-98. About 1892, he also built a two-storey house in Merritton for his wife and five daughters, but it, like his carriage, became an unfortunate victim of the Merritton Tornado of 1898. The old farmhouse was picked up in the wind storm and deposited on the opposite side of the road, leaving it in a shambles. While three of the Thompson family had been in the house at the time, fortunately no one was killed. With $800 in tornado relief aid provided as a victim of the storm, Richard personally rebuilt the house on the foundation of the old to the same design. However, he never attempted to make another self-propelled vehicle. The Thompson family (seen above) moved into their new home on December 24, 1898, and gave thanks for their many blessings. The Thompsons moved to Oakdale Avenue near Merritt Street about 1913. It is not known what happened to their old Smythe Street home.

WILLIAM ABBEY HOME, *c.*1900
28 Bayview Dr. (formerly Albert St., cor. of Elgin)

William S. Abbey moved into this Port Dalhousie home in 1898. He was a carpenter by trade. He continued to reside there until around 1923. Abbey was an important name in Port Dalhousie – Abbey Bros. (John P. and James S.) operated a shipyard on Lake Ontario, just west of Lock 1 of the First Welland Canal. They later carried on their shipbuilding business in Port Robinson. One of William's relations, Mrs. Rachel Abbey, inherited the house in 1927. The home's wood siding has since been stuccoed, the chimneys are gone, and the detailing has been removed from above and around the porch. In June 1961 the street was renamed, from Albert to Bayview, after the Town's amalgamation into the larger City of St. Catharines. In total, 100 streets were renamed to eliminate duplication.

CRAWFORD HOME, *c.*1906-07
46 Bayview Dr. (formerly Albert St.) • (demolished *c.*1979)

Crawford was an old family name in Port Dalhousie for at least half a century. Mrs. Margaret Crawford, widow of James, lived on Bayview Drive from 1881 until 1931. Lucy Crawford, the widow of George B. Crawford and the mother of George Ralston Crawford, lived in this Bayview Drive house in 1955 and 1956. George Crawford was a shoemaker and Great Lakes ship captain. George and Lucy had previously lived on Main Street between 1904 and 1911, at about which time the family moved to Buffalo. Their son, Ralston, was born in St. Catharines in 1906. He was an accomplished artist who became famous for his Precisionist paintings and lithographs of machines, especially boats, docks, shipyards, and bridges. Ralston Crawford died in 1978 in New Orleans and was buried with a full brass-band funeral. The Bayview Drive house was vacant in 1979 before being demolished and replaced by a new brick bungalow at #46 by the Conn family.

MAY-CLARK HOME (*Walnut Dale Farm*), *c.*1925
3 Sparkes St. • Built: *c.*1790 (destroyed by fire 1984)

After the American Revolution, William May, a former Butler's Ranger, settled in Upper Canada as a United Empire Loyalist. He was given a 282.8-hectare (700 acre) land grant, on which he built his Georgian-style home in 1790. William May Sr. died in 1827 and the property passed to his grandson, William May Jr. (son of John). In 1838, he sold the home to Lt.-Col. John Clark who named the property *Walnut Dale Farm*. Clark was the area Customs Collector and a secretary of the original Welland Canal Company. Upon his death in 1862, the home passed through a succession of owners, including the Coles, Beltons, Sparkes (Mary E. Sparkes is in the photo), and the Seilers, who bought the property in 1961. Hermann and Inge Seiler built a new home to the west of the old, and in the early 1980s, a group of community volunteers came together as Heritage St. Catharines to restore the home as a centre for historical interpretation. All plans came to an abrupt end when a suspicious fire destroyed the building on "Devil's Night," October 30, 1984.

Four
Commercial/Industrial
The Downtown

THOS. PAGET GARAGE, 1927
42 Geneva St. (cor. of Niagara) • (demolished c.1949-50)

Thomas Paget operated the St. Catharines Tire Company from 42 Geneva Street from 1920 through 1928. The business was located in a uniquely shaped building at the tip of land in front of the present site of the Central Fire Hall. In the background is the Wise Lumber Company. Tom (*l*), and his son, Tom Paget Jr. (*r*), sold Good Year tires, gas (from the gravity pump on the left), oils, greases, and batteries, and, if you had "Tire Trouble", they were only a phone call away at #1102. Ernie Wilson, standing between the Pagets in this photo, was their salesman. From 1929 to 1932, the Pagets sold tires at 8 Queenston Street. Tom Jr. then carried on at 30 Queenston Street from 1933-37. The building at 42 Geneva Street was still there in 1949 and appears to have been demolished to make way for the Central Fire Hall that was built in 1950.

FORMER NIAGARA DISTRICT/IMPERIAL BANK, *c.*1950
5 St. Paul Cres. • (demolished 1956)

St. Catharines is considered the birthplace of the Canadian Imperial Bank of Commerce (CIBC). The Niagara District Bank, established in 1853 by William Hamilton Merritt, was merged with the Imperial Bank of Canada in 1875, which itself amalgamated with the Canadian Bank of Commerce in 1961 to form the present Canadian Imperial Bank of Commerce (CIBC). Thomas Rodman Merritt and Senator James Rae Benson were both on the original Board of Directors of the Imperial. The Bank building, by then apartments, was demolished in 1956 when the Canadian Oil Companies bought the land. That station has since been replaced by a commercial plaza built at what is now 5 St. Paul Crescent, and occupied by Sally McGarr Realty and other local businesses.

MIKE McGUIRE STORE, 1933
29 St. Paul Cres. • Built: 1860s (demolished)

Although it was probably built in the early 1860s, Mike McGuire did not come into ownership of this store until the late 1870s. Although it was originally a grocery, McGuire used the premises as a second-hand store until 1933 when it closed. Wooden sidewalks can be seen in front of the shop while St. Paul Crescent drops off to the right down to Twelve Mile Creek. The building has been demolished.

PRENDERGAST BLOCK, *c.*1900
23 St. Paul St. • Built: 1850 (demolished 1949) • Architect: Kivas Tully (Toronto)

Located at the corner of St. Paul and William Streets, the Prendergast Block was one of the most elegant business and office blocks in St. Catharines. Built in the Renaissance Revival style, the building featured stone-fronted façades and gables, and other details similar to those found on Rodman Hall, built in 1853. The building, originally owned by William Hamilton Merritt, was named after his wife's family name, "Prendergast". It contained over 2323 m^2 (25,000 s.f.) of floor area, most of which was occupied by James D. Tait's dry goods store, the largest (and often considered the best) in the Niagara Region. Tait died in 1907 and in 1934 his portion of the Block was taken over by Mr. A.M. Stobie dry goods and later by appliance dealer, Hunter and Son. It was purchased in 1945 by the S.S. Kresge Company Limited and was demolished in 1949 to make way for Kresge's. The building was later occupied by the United Way, and is presently (2005) home to the Mai Vi restaurant serving Vietnamese cuisine.

T. Eaton Co. Ltd., 1978
15-31 St. Paul St. • Built: 1936-37
(demolished 1978) • Architect: Samuel H. Maw

The T. Eaton Company purchased McLaren's dry goods store at the corner of St. Paul and William Streets in the early 1920s to establish a branch of the Canadian Department Stores (CDS was a division of Eaton's). The original three-storey building was destroyed by fire in March 1936, and was replaced with the two-storey brick building seen here. It opened in January 1937 and stood for 41 years until demolished in 1978 to make way for the One St. Paul Street office-retail complex. Eaton's opened at the Pen Centre on Easter Monday 1973 (April 23rd). The local store of the financially troubled retailer closed in October 1999.

W.W. Walker & Sons, Florist, 1956
156 St. Paul St. (renumbered to 156 from 81 St. Paul Street in 1932)

In 1903, when he was 21, William Wallace Walker left his job at the Port Dalhousie Canning Factory to pursue a career as a florist. His first greenhouse was located on Queenston Street. In 1952, the business moved to 156 St. Paul Street. Walker was particularly famous for his orchids, owning one of the biggest orchid lots in Canada. Walker sent his orchids to such people as Bette Davis, Dwight D. Eisenhower, Elizabeth, the Queen Mother, Sir Anthony Eden, and Sir Winston Churchill. After his death in 1968, William Wallace's sons continued the business, with William Jr. in charge of the retail operations and John managing the greenhouses. Their greenhouses, which were located at 260 St. Paul Street W. since 1962, closed in 1972.

F.W. WOOLWORTH CO. / DIANA SWEETS, c. 1950
107-115 St. Paul St. (renumbered in 1932 from #61-67)

In 1914, the Woolworth Company scouted St. Catharines with plans to open a new "5, 10 and 15 cent store." They chose a location on the north side of St. Paul Street in the block between Queen Street and Helliwell's Lane. Woolworth's occupied the ground floor of a two-storey building to the left (#105, not visible), plus, partially extended into the main floor of the three-storey structure seen here. The F.W. Woolworth Company closed in 1963. Next door, Greek immigrant Peter Grammar established the highly popular Diana Sweets in 1920 as an ice cream parlour and candy shop. It was remodelled in 1926 and again in 1935 to include light lunches and full-course meals. The eatery's famous gumwood booths and traditional soda fountain were still in place when "The Di" closed on March 16, 1996. The location has since been occupied by a variety of small businesses and in 2005 was home to Kaz's Pub and Shtoynkas Sandwiches.

THE HIPPODROME THEATRE, 1909
118-116, 114 St. Paul St. (later occupied by #174-172, 170) • Built: 1907 (demolished 1922)

The Hippodrome on St. Paul Street played host to several different types of theatre, including vaudeville acts and moving pictures, such as the "thrilling western drama, *A Nugget of Gold*", advertised on the portico. Misfortune struck the theatre in 1908, only one year after it opened, when a fire ravaged the building. It was rebuilt within a year (shown here), however, its renewed life was short-lived. The Hippodrome was levelled in 1922 when dry-goods merchant Ralph J. Hoffman bought the site and built a ladies' apparel store. Various businesses have since occupied that building, including Holly's Candy Store, Susan Miles Ltd., and in 2005, the Oasis restaurant serving Middle East Cuisine.

Sovereign Bank of Canada, 1907
185 St. Paul St. (cor. of James, renumbered in 1932 from #113-115) • Built: 1907 (demolished 1966) • Architect: H.C. Stone (Montreal) • Builder: Newman Bros. (StC)

The Sovereign Bank of Canada, established in 1901, built this imposing structure in 1907 for its St. Catharines banking operations. However, before it even got a chance to open it was taken over by the Bank of Nova Scotia. By January 1908, the parent bank – because of its zealous pursuit of business – had accumulated a substantial number of bad loan accounts. It was arranged that its liabilities would be guaranteed by twelve of the major banks at the time, and it would liquidate its affairs. The 1907 *Standard* referred to it as "The handsomest office building in St. Catharines." They also stated that it occupied "one of the most important corners in the city." Offices occupied the upper floors of the four-storey structure. The Bank relocated to temporary quarters in 1966 while the old building was torn down and a new one built (which officially opened on March 1, 1968).

RUSSELL HOUSE HOTEL, *c.*1932-38
201-207 St. Paul St. (renumbered in 1932 from #137-139, cor. of James) • Built: *c.*1843 (demolished 1996) • Designated: 1986 (de-designated 1989)

The Russell Hotel, or Russell House as it was originally known, was built for Samuel Stinson, and was most likely used as a tavern. After Samuel Stinson was killed by his wife in 1846, his son Francis took ownership and started a grocery store on the ground floor. The building has had several owners since then, including James Cairn, John Quinn, John O'Keefe, Emery Sargeant, and Jerry Kowal. The interior was ravaged by fire in 1996. After its demolition, the site became an outdoor patio, but is now a vacant lot. The distinctive stained glass and neon-illuminated canopy sign over the St. Paul Street entrance has been restored for display at the St. Catharines Museum.

GRAND CENTRAL HOTEL, *c.*1880
288 St. Paul Street (renumbered in 1932 from #184-194/200) • Built: 1877

The stately Grand Central Hotel featured a gabled roof and wrought-iron balconies. It was later known as the Lincoln. In 1971, the three-storey building was bought by the Toronto-based Kennash Corporation, and turned into the Montebello Inn. The new hotel was completely modernized with new bars, retiled floors, and the removal of the sweeping staircase that had characterized the inside of the building. The remodelling was intended to give the place a "Las Vegas look." In 2005, the modernized building no longer serves as a hotel but is a mix of offices on the upper floors and retail ("Sal's Place" clothing) and a restaurant (Sahla Thai) at the street level.

St. Paul Street Businesses, *c.*1914
296-298 St Paul St. (renumbered in 1932 from #196-198) • (demolished)

At the time of this photograph, this commercial complex was shared by William A. Hill's "Grand Central" barbershop and Roy E. Clapp's plumbing and sheet metal business. From 1931 to 1946, #298 St. Paul was occupied by William G. Watson, tailor. In 1947, Jack Nash Men's Wear opened in the former Watson tailor premises. At its peak, the store employed twenty workers. The business was taken over by Harold and Maurice Nash after the death of their father in 1962. After the custom tailoring side of the business was discontinued, they also expanded into women's clothing and occupied #296-302 St. Paul Street. The store had become one of the preferred clothing shops in the downtown. A Grantham Plaza location was opened about 1968, managed today by Dave Nash, grandson of the business founder. The St. Paul Street store closed in 1991. The building has been demolished and replaced by a parking lot.

F.C. BURROUGHES FURNITURE, c.1930
421-429, 431 St. Paul St. (renumbered in 1932 from #273-277)

The F.C. Burroughes Furniture Store had locations in Toronto, Brantford, Niagara Falls, and St. Catharines. When they first established business in St. Catharines in 1928, the Burroughes company was located at the corner of St. Paul and Court Streets, as per this photo. They also had a main warehouse on the south side of Permilla Street. Note the automobile parked out front in the days when there was two-way traffic on St. Paul Street (changed to one-way in July 11, 1954). In 1933, a "removal sale" was held at the Burroughes store (they moved to #316-322 on the opposite side of St. Paul Street near Bond Street). Phillips Department Store then occupied the premises until 1937 when it became an A&P grocery store. The A&P was there until 1967 (when it relocated to the Midtown Plaza on Welland Avenue). By 1969 it was the Twin Fair Department Store and from 1973 has been home to Dr. Ivan Hrabowsky's Downtown Dental Centre. The building received a heritage award in 1976 for its sympathetic restoration.

YMCA, BET. 1906-28
259 St. Paul St. (renumbered in 1932 from #165,167) • Built: 1906 (demolished 1928)

YMCAs in Canada began in 1851. James Mills organized the first YMCA in St. Catharines in 1859. Its headquarters was established in rented rooms on Hainer Street. In 1891, the society reorganized and opened at 33 Queen Street, across from the old Post Office. This neo-Romanesque building on St. Paul Street – containing a gymnasium, bowling alley, and library – was opened in 1906. Operations continued there until 1928 when a new building was opened at 56 Queen Street. The St. Paul Street location was demolished to make way for the Leonard Hotel.

YM-YWCA, *c.*1945
56 Queen St. • Built: 1928 (demolished 1994) • Architect: Nicholson & Macbeth (StC)

It was decided to build a new 'Y' after the St. Paul Street building became increasingly outmoded. A successful public subscription campaign, which enabled the project to proceed, included two generous donations from local philanthropists – one from David Bloss Mills, and the other a $100,000 contribution from Reuben Wells Leonard. The new YMCA on Queen Street, built in the Neo-Tudor style, opened one year prior to the YWCA's 1929 formation in St. Catharines. For a while, both groups shared the same building, the first combined YM-YWCA in North America. The handsome building was demolished in 1994 after the new Walker YMCA was built on YMCA Drive.

KEATING BUILDING, *c*.1895
38-36-34 Queen St. (renumbered *c*.1898-1904 from #35) • (demolished)

Michael Y. Keating sold books and stationery on the ground floor of this three-storey brick building, established about 1885. It was known as the "Post Office Book Store," being adjacent to the old Post Office at the corner of Queen and King Streets. Keating was very involved in the community and served as Mayor from 1899-1900, represented St. Andrew's Ward on City Council, and was a Trustee for both the St. Catharines General & Marine Hospital and the Roman Catholic Separate School Board (where he also served as Secretary-Treasurer). He was also a Justice of the Peace, sat on the Board of Trade, and served as a Director of the Security Loan and Savings Co. In this photo, Nassau W. Gowan's Dominion Music Store occupies the storefront on the right. It appears as if a new shipment of crated pianos has just been dropped off from the Dominion Organ and Piano Co. of Bowmanville. Gowan also gained fame in marine circles as the inventor of the "Gowan Safety Device," which, when mounted to the gates of the locks of the Third Canal, prevented their accidental opening if struck by a ship. Keating died in 1917 at age 83, and Gowan died in 1924 at age 68. The building has been demolished.

THE STANDARD, *c.*1900
17-21 Queen St.

The Daily Standard produced its first edition on April 21, 1891. At the time it was one of three papers in St. Catharines. After only one year of publication, the paper had acquired sizeable debts and was facing bankruptcy. William B. Burgoyne was the paper's mechanical superintendent. He purchased the paper, and all of its debts, for $1. He was a capable newspaper man, being in the printing business since 1868 and with the *Evening Star* at the time of its founding in 1886. Under his direction, *The Standard* flourished. In 1898 this building on Queen Street was purchased. By 1920 the other papers, *The Star* and *The Journal*, had ceased publishing, and *The Standard* had a monopoly on the business. In 1912, the paper purchased its first delivery van. In 1913 a rotary press was installed in the building, and in 1929 it acquired a 32-page press. The building itself was revamped in 1950, and expanded in 1973, occupying several conjoined buildings between Queen and William Streets. The paper remained family owned until sold to Southam in 1996. At the time it was one of the largest privately operated papers in Canada. CanWest Global acquired it in 2001, and since 2003 the paper has been part of the Osprey Media Group.

ERNEST PENNER INC., *c.*1985
53 Queen St. • Built: pre-1852

Ernest Penner opened his jewellery business on St. Paul Street in 1970, moving six years later to this newly renovated building at 53 Queen Street. Prior to that, it had been a residence, owned by several individuals, including Robert Richmond (1836-54), William Greenwood (1854-55), Ann Hardy (1855-93), and James Prior (1893-1941), the owner of Dominion Hair Cloth. It was converted into an apartment complex during the Second World War. Under Penner's ownership, the building became one of St. Catharines' premier jewellery stores. It was again renovated in 1995, with the addition of a library containing books about jewellery, and a new entrance, converted from one of the windows, featuring columns and a small portico.

PHELAN'S PARK GROCERY, 1930
74-74½ Queen St. • Architect: Thomas H. Wiley (StC)

The Sullivan Block at the corner of Queen, Lake, and Duke Streets included a combination of grocery, pharmacy, and variety store businesses. Phelan's Grocery occupied the premises for 23 years, replacing an earlier grocer, M.J. Kane. Known as the "Upper" Phelan, to distinguish his business from a second Phelan's Grocery at the corner of Queen and Welland, Phelan shared the street floor with Robert M. Black, who was a druggist there between 1929-30, and later a representative for the Canada Life Assurance Co. To the left under the awning was a barbershop, later occupied by a rare books dealer. Phelan himself moved out of the complex in 1933, although the other Phelan grocery remained in operation until 1992. From the 1930s through 1978, Italian-born Joseph Sciamanda operated the Park Fruit Store. Avondale has been there since 1972. In addition to the ground floor commercial uses, the building contains four apartments.

H.E. Rose & Co., *c.*1938
3-5 Queen St. • (demolished)

The 18-year old Howard Rose founded the H.E. Rose Company in 1910. The company handled real estate, loans, insurance, investments, and securities. Rose later became an alderman of St. Catharines, and president of the St. Catharines Rotary Club. The insurance company of H.E. Rose, which became Rose, Horne & Stevenson Insurance Ltd. in 1967, operated from this Queen Street location from 1930 until 1968, when they moved to 12 King Street. They remained there for seven years before moving to 71 King Street. In 1995, the company made a fourth move, to 63 Church Street. The original Queen Street building was replaced by a branch of the Royal Bank of Canada (now RBC Financial Services).

A.A. Widdicombe and Son Frigidaire, 1955
67 Ontario St.

Arthur A. Widdicombe was initially employed as an upholsterer in the local plant of the Reo Motor Car Company. After the plant's closure in 1913, he established an auto parts store on the corner of Ontario and Trafalgar. He started out selling radiator covers, car tops, and upholstery, but eventually gave up this business to start one of the largest and most successful appliance, refrigeration, and air conditioning firms in the Niagara Peninsula. In 1927, Widdicombe purchased the Frigidaire franchise in St. Catharines, which he operated from the same Ontario Street building along with his son, Donald W. Widdicombe. Note the old Red Ensign flag atop the store, the 1955 Ford panel truck, and the advertisement for the "Boy Scout's [World] Jamboree" being held in Niagara-on-the-Lake in 1955. Widdicombe's closed in 1977. The Widdicombe building is now part of the Durward, Jones, Barkwell chartered accounting offices.

WELLAND HOUSE HOTEL, *c.*1947
30 Ontario St. • Built: 1853-56 • Architect: John Latshaw (Drummondville/NF) • Builder: John Clyde (StC)

The mineral waters of St. Catharines were thought to possess particularly beneficial properties for treating rheumatism, gout, and skin and internal diseases. Several spas opened in St. Catharines, including the Welland House. When it first opened, the Welland House had no access to an artesian well, but piped its mineral waters from near the Stephenson House (they later drilled their own well at the hotel). The Welland House was the tallest building in St. Catharines at the time of its construction. The hotel operated under several owners, many of whom undertook renovations to the historic property. In the late 1920s L.B. Spencer upgraded the hotel with marquees, a drug store, a dining room lined with Florida Cypress, and chandeliers from Toronto's Casa Loma. The baths were closed in 1941, but the Welland continued to operate as a hotel until the early 1990s. It was converted into a residence for university students about 1994.

ONTARIO STREET BUSINESSES, 1975
31-33-35 Ontario St. • Built: *c.*1850

Originally owned by Jedediah P. Merritt, this Ontario Street structure saw many changes in ownership and usage. In 1874, the Montreal Telegraph Company was located there, and in the early 1900s, Welsh & Company Wholesale Grocers owned the building. The Grocers remained until 1961, and the building had a four-year vacancy. From 1965 to 1974, the building was used as a temporary headquarters for various charities. Today, access to apartments on the upper floors is provided through the central door, #33, while inventory for the Sleep Factory flanks each side.

GRAND OPERA HOUSE, 1907
43-45-47-49-51 Ontario St. (#47 is the entrance to the Grand Opera House) • (demolished 1992/1998)

Sometimes referred to as the Grand Opera House, this row of shops on Ontario Street was actually home to a print shop and a broker at the time of this photo. Access to the richly decorated Opera House theatre in the rear was a long entrance through 47 Ontario Street, shown here under a sign for "The Grand," and thence through a connecting building to the actual theatre. The Grand opened in 1877 and was twice damaged by fire, once in 1895, then a second time in 1926. The theatre was closed after the second fire, but later converted into a bowling alley, Dorado Lanes. After another fire, in late 1992 the remains of the entry building were demolished down to the first floor. The space was later replaced by a parking lot. The actual Opera House building, located on the lane behind, survived another six years until it too succumbed to the wrecker's ball.

KING GEORGE THEATRE, 1917
38 James St. (renumbered in 1930 from #20) • Built: 1915 • Architect: Thomas H. Wiley (StC)

Thomas McIlwain, the owner (back seat) and Leo Coyle, the manager (front passenger seat) of the King George Theatre until 1936, charged only ten cents admission to see films like the dramatic *The Price of Silence*, advertised here. After 1936 the theatre was known as the Granada, and in 1947 was again renamed, becoming the Park Theatre. The television age dawned in the 1950s, drawing to a close the golden age of movie theatres. Sadly, the Park was shut down in 1956. Station to Station and Williams Jewellers occupy the premises as of 2005.

IOOF Union Lodge #16, 1924
36, 34-28 James St. (renumbered in 1930 from #20) • Architect: Nicholson & Macbeth (StC)

Union Lodge #16, IOOF (Independent Order of Oddfellows) was built in the neo-Tudor style. The original #16 Lodge, formed in 1846, was located at the corner of James and St. Paul Streets until destroyed by fire in 1858. The replacement Lodge on the second floor of 13 Ontario Street was also demolished, this time to make way for a St. Paul Street extension to the new Burgoyne Bridge. Union Lodge #16 shared a temporary home with the Oddfellows Empire Lodge #87 at 17 Queen Street until their new building was completed. The photograph depicts the laying of the cornerstone in April 1924 at the Union Lodge's present James Street location. J.E. Anderson, Grand Master of the Province of Ontario, dedicated the building on November 24, 1924. Four retail businesses occupy the ground level while the IOOF Temple and offices are on the upper two floors.

Payne's Meat Market, 1978
100 King St. • (demolished c.1978)

Since the early decades of the 20th century, businesses in the building at 100 King Street offered fresh meat and produce from a local butcher or grocer. From 1917 to 1925 The Carry Market butchers occupied the premises. In 1926, the building was purchased by Kenneth Vine, who continued the business as a butcher shop with a particular reputation as a pork-packing house. After Vine's departure in 1931, the store remained vacant for two years until Carroll's Ltd. grocery opened in 1934. The grocery remained until 1952, when Hocking's Meat Market took over the shop. From 1971 until 1977, Payne's Meat Market occupied the premises. It was vacant in 1978 and seems to have been torn down by the following year. As of 2005, the site of the former Meat Market is an outdoor patio for Stella's restaurant. To the left in the photo is the Star Restaurant, now the Astoria Restaurant.

Moyer Bro's Flour and Feed, c.1920s
127-129 King St. (renumbered c.1924-25 from #57-59)

When miller Lewis Moyer opened Moyer Bro's Flour and Feed at 57 King Street about 1914, he began a tradition of feed stores that would continue in that building for almost eighty years. Moyer Bros. operated until about 1924, when it became the St. Catharines Feed Barn (later located at the corner of King and James). About 1925, the store again changed hands to become the Sparks and Byers Flour & Feed store, which remained until about 1934 when it became the Byers Feed and Seed Co. Byers ceased operations by 1990. In 2005 the building was occupied by the Cremation Centre Inc. (#127) and Synergy Benefits Consulting Inc. (#129).

TOM MATTHEWS BLACKSMITH SHOP, 1950
Garden Park (formerly 36 Mary St.) • Built: 1860s-70s (demolished)

This building was first located on Lyman Street and was reportedly a residence for the priests of St. Catherine of Alexandria Roman Catholic Church. Its next use was as St. Bridget's Separate School. When the Church decided in 1892 to build a new, brick school on the same site, the old frame school was divided in two and relocated a half block south to the east side of Mary Street. This lot would one day be in the vicinity of the St. Catharines Public Library. The building was used for Lowe and Boylan's carriage factory until it was purchased in 1915 by E.B. Wills who made delivery wagons for dairies. After 18 years, the business was taken over by Tom Matthews. He had a blacksmith shop across the street at #35. He moved the blacksmith shop into 36 Mary Street to combine it with the wagon-building business. The business lasted until 1950 and the building has since been demolished.

CORBLOC, 1974
80 King St. • Built: 1974 • Architect: Eberhard H. Zeidler (Toronto)

Corbloc cost more than $10,000,000 when built in 1974. A number of old buildings and long-standing shops were razed and replaced with the modern ten-storey complex. Many had hoped that it would help rejuvenate the downtown but it was not the complete success that had been expected. The building was bought in 2003 by Hughson Business of Hamilton and as of the fall of 2005 was undergoing an extensive renovation program.

LINCOLN TRUST HOUSE, 1974
60 James St. • Built: 1974 • Architect: Donald Chapman (NF)

The Lincoln Trust House is located on the former site of the Murray House Hotel, built in 1864, and named after Capt. James Murray. After a change in ownership in 1868, the building was renamed the Pickwick House, under which name it remained for five years before returning to its previous name. The building was renovated in 1900, becoming the New Murray Hotel. It continued to be known as the New Murray until demolished to make way for the Lincoln Trust building in 1974. Lincoln Trust was absorbed by Canada Trust in 1977 and the name of the new building was subsequently changed. A branch of the merged TD-Canada Trust Company was there until about 2004. As of 2005, small offices occupy the fourth and fifth floors, while the Region Niagara Community Services and Province of Ontario Early Childhood offices take up the first three floors.

KARN BROTHERS GROCERY, BET. 1911-65
62 Welland Ave. • Built: *c.*1872

The original survey pattern used for Grantham Township was north-south, and *roughly* east-west, but parallel to Lake Ontario. The street layout created rhomboid-patterned blocks, resulting in some uniquely shaped intersections and buildings, such as the unusual six-sided one shown here. Located at the three-way intersection of Welland, Lake, and James Streets, the Karn brothers, Harry and Charles, operated their grocery store here from 1911 until 1965. Upon closing, it became Hansa Imports, followed by a sub shop. It has been Forget-Me-Knot Antiques and Alice's Antiques since 1993.

Springbank Hotel, *c.*1894
Yates St. (e.s. nr. College) • Built: 1864-65 (destroyed by fire 1903)

The Springbank Hotel was built with "Victorian spaciousness" by Dr. Theophilus Mack. Mack was previously associated with the Stephenson House Hotel, but left because of the questionable curative claims they were making. Dr. Mack's new spa hotel was a four-storey, red-brick structure, with fountains and plantings adorning the creek-side slope. The building was expanded in 1869, with an extra wing containing a billiard room, new bathrooms, and water tanks. A further 279m^2 (3000 s.f.) were added in 1873. Though the Springbank offered the popular mineral baths, as did the Stephenson House and the Welland House hotels, it operated more like a sanatorium with nursing care and massage therapy. The Springbank remained open until Dr. Mack's death in 1881. In 1888, the closed building was sold to the founders of Bishop Ridley College, which opened the following year in the renovated former spa hotel. While the Springbank was the last to open, it was the first of the three famous spas to close. The main building burned down in 1903 with only the former laundry (later the school gymnasium) remaining. This has been converted into three elegant townhouses at #62-64-66 Yates Street.

SILVERWOOD'S DAIRY, 1977
277 Welland Ave. • (demolished c.1980)

Opened in 1923, for the next forty years Silverwood's Dairy provided area homes with pasteurized milk, cream, buttermilk, butter, and ice cream. At first located at 6 Queenston Street, the business moved to 277 Welland Avenue about 1929 where they remained until closing about 1972. An entrance to a central courtyard of the dairy was provided by means of a porte-cochère through the Welland Avenue façade. Demolished about 1980, the site was replaced with a commercial plaza about 1983. During Silverwood's period of local operation, some of the other dairies which served St. Catharines included: Sunshine, Sanitary, Mason's, McMahon's, Garden City, Ernest Cain, E.A. Bunting, and Avondale (the only dairy still existing after 1973).

TAYLOR AND BATE BREWERY, 1928
Brewery St. (e.s.) • (demolished 1979)

James Taylor established his brewery in St. Catharines in an era when many towns boasted their own breweries. Located on the banks of Twelve Mile Creek, the original building was destroyed by fire in 1839 after only five years of operation, but it was quickly rebuilt. In 1857, Taylor was joined by a business partner, Thomas B. Bate. After their deaths (Taylor in 1886, Bate in 1901), the family partnership continued under their several sons. The brewery ran under the Taylor and Bate name for 63 years, until it was sold in 1927 to E.T. Sandell who later operated the local radio station, CKTB (some say this was an acronym for a "Cold Keg of Taylor and Bate" or "Canadians Know Their Beer"). In the late 1930s the business was sold a second time, to E.P. Taylor's Brewing Corporation of Canada (later called Carling-O'Keefe), who owned it for only a short period of time before the brewery was permanently closed due to the Depression economy. The building was demolished in 1979 to make way for Highway 406.

LINCOLN FOUNDRY, c.1979
65 St. Paul Cres. (below Burgoyne Bridge) • (demolished c.1979)

Operated since 1867 as the Norris Roller Mills, this building on the bank of the Twelve Mile Creek became Kinleith Paper in 1900. Edward and William Finlay from Scotland brought their papermaking skills to St. Catharines and supervised the establishment of the mill. The mill produced fine papers, such as writing, book, and lithograph papers. It operated until 1927, though the building suffered a major disaster when a rag boiler exploded in 1904. In 1939, Louis Burnstein and A.E. Coleman established the Lincoln Foundry, which produced cast iron parts until 1979. The building was demolished and the site cleared in preparation for construction of Highway 406.

CONROY MANUFACTURING CO., 1930s
55 Catherine St. • Built *c.*1938

In 1913, John Conroy moved to St. Catharines from Port Hope and established a factory to undertake custom machining. Originally named Andert and Conroy, the factory's name changed in 1920 to Conroy Manufacturing and Tool, and then to Conroy Manufacturing Company Limited in 1924. The company manufactured a variety of products through the years including auto parts, oil and gas furnaces (they were one of the largest in Canada), hardware for transmission lines (withcustomers in India, Spain, and Scotland), and all of the outdoor switching equipment used on the Welland Ship Canal. John Conroy purchased William Andert's shares in 1925, and the following year, took on Harry J. Carmichael as a partner (in which capacity he remained until 1965). In 1966, Conroy's was purchased by Kelsey Wheel, renamed Kelsey-Hayes the following year. Theyconverted the plant to make auto parts. Kelsey-Hayes ceased operations in 1995. The striking Art Deco designed building has been occupied by Hamdani Enterprises since about 1997-98.

McKinnon Industries Ltd., 1938
Ontario St. (s. of Carlton St.) • Architect: Thomas H. Wiley (StC) • Builder: Newman Bros. (StC)

In 1876, Lachlan Ebenezer McKinnon and F.F. Mitchell opened a hardware store on St. Paul Street. In 1888 the business had expanded and became McKinnon Dash & Hardware Co., specializing in carriage dashes. Another thirteen years saw yet another major expansion with the opening of the Ontario Street foundry. During the First World War, they produced saddles, harnesses, and shells for the Allies. Following the War, the company turned its production to auto parts, attracting as its largest client, General Motors of Canada. Six years after the death of Lachlan McKinnon, the company joined the General Motors group as a largely owned subsidiary (1929), still retaining the McKinnon name. Its name was changed to General Motors on February 1, 1969.

NEELON MILL, c.1885
13 Race St. • Built: 1882 (demolished 1965)

In 1882, Capt. Sylvester Neelon purchased the frame Red Mill originally owned by Oliver Phelps and William Hamilton Merritt, tore it down and constructed a new stone grist mill. The new mill operated until 1895 when the Packard Electric Co. purchased it. They converted it to a factory to produce lamps, motors, and transformers. Packard abandoned the building shortly after its amalgamation with the Ferranti Electric Company Ltd. in 1958. Ferranti-Packard built a new factory on Dieppe Road, and in 1965 the Neelon Mill was demolished. The original inscribed cornerstone was preserved and moved to Ferranti-Packard's new location on Dieppe Road.

Five
Commercial/Industrial
Grantham/Homer/ Merritton/Port Dalhousie

WHITMAN AND BARNES KNIFE WORKS, c.1890
90 Oakdale Ave. (formerly Thorold Rd.) • Built: 1870 (destroyed by fire 1997)

This building was constructed in 1870 on the site of the original Riordon Paper Mill. It was taken over by the Canada Knife Works in 1874. In six years, it was known as the Whitman and Barnes Knife Works, managed by George Burtch and Samuel Collinson. The company, which also had branches in the United States, France, and England, manufactured blades for tools, including mowers, reapers, binder straw cutters, and planers. The company existed until shortly after the First World War when it was bought by McKinnon Industries Ltd. and the manufacturing equipment was removed. The building, heavily damaged by fire on April 16, 1966, was salvaged and renovated in 1986-87 by the Welland Canals Preservation Association and the Welland Canals Society. In February 1997, it was again ruined by fire and subsequently demolished.

St. Catharines Golf Club – Club House, *c*.1919
70 Westchester Cr.

The first two golf courses in St. Catharines, the St. Catharines Golf Club and the Alexandra Golf Club (located on the Ridley College grounds), opened in 1899 and 1902, respectively. In 1909, due to lack of space, the two courses merged into the St. Catharines Golf Club on Westchester Avenue. Originally a nine-hole course, in 1947 the grounds were renovated by Stanley Thompson and the golfing legend, Robert Trent Jones, and converted into an 18-hole course. The new grounds reopened on June 12, 1949. Further alterations to the course were made in 1963 to make room for Highway 406. This was funded by the Province of Ontario.

QUEENSTON STREET GREENHOUSES, c.1900
104 Queenston St.

In 1863, John Holder established the Rosebank Nursery with a greenhouse at 102 Queenston Street, probably the first commercial greenhouse in St. Catharines. His dahlias, gladioli, fuchsias, cucumbers, strawberries, and rhubarb were all regular prize winners at area horticultural shows. About 1889, Robert Lance Dunn had started in business, and from 1895 had a 'hot-bed sash' operation on Trafalgar near Ontario Street. R.L. Dunn purchased the Queenston Street property in 1900 and moved there in 1902. His specialty was cut flowers, roses, carnations, palms, and flowering plants grown under glass in his 5000 square feet of greenhouses. Four generations of Dunns have fulfilled the floral needs of the community. Their store still operates from 106 Queenston Street.

LIGHTNING FASTENER CO. LTD., 1925
50 Niagara St. (cor. of Davidson St.) • Built: 1925

Early versions of fasteners were developed and patented in the United States, most notably in 1851 by Elias Howe and in 1893/1905 by Whitcomb L. Judson. However, it was the Swedish-American Gideon Sundback (photo upper right, facing left), who is credited as the "Inventor of the Zipper". He not only designed the first successful slide fastener (later referred to as the modern zipper), with a system of interlocking teeth and scoops, but also developed a machine in 1913, later improved upon, for mass-producing his invention. Seen here is the cornerstone laying ceremony for Sundback's new Lightning Fastener building in St. Catharines, 1925.

LIGHTNING FASTENER CO. LTD., 1937
50 Niagara St. • Built: 1925

Gideon Sundback (front row, seventh from the left) established the Lightning Fastener Company in St. Catharines in 1925. He commuted to St. Catharines every Monday from Meadville, Pennsylvania, where he maintained his permanent residence. The company merged with Talon in 1947. Textron then acquired Talon U.S. and its foreign subsidiaries, including Lightning Fastener, in 1968. The U.S. firm, NuCon Holdings Inc., purchased the Talon, Lightning, and all Talon subsidiaries in April of 1981, closing the St. Catharines and Montreal operations in October of the same year. The building now houses various small businesses.

Empire Rug Mills, 1937
5-7 Frank St. (cor. Gale Cr.) • Built: 1903

From 1903 until 1921, this building housed the businesses of several builders and contractors. The Empire Rug Mills were located there from 1927 until its closure in 1970. The rug maker was first located at 90 Queenston Street (in 1925 and 1926). The Frank Street operations of the Empire Rug Mills included weaving, finishing, examination, storage and shipping facilities. This was not the first rug maker to use the "Empire" name in St. Catharines. The Etherington Brothers moved their Empire Carpet Works from Paris to St. Catharines in 1891, setting up business in a plant at the corner of Welland Avenue and Catherine Street. It was destroyed by fire in June 1903. It is not known if there was any connection between the two businesses bearing the Empire name.

Foster Wheeler, c.1950
81 Eastchester Ave.

Foster Wheeler considered moving into the Westchester area as early as 1907, but lacked financing for such a plan until 1927 when the company took over the Jenckes Engineering and Machine Works of Canada. Foster Wheeler manufactured large industrial equipment and machinery for pulp mills. At the time of the Second World War, it was St. Catharines' third largest factory – employing over 140 citizens in its boiler shop, machine shop, and foundry – producing, among other things, boilers for naval corvettes. The Eastchester Avenue plant closed in 1997 and Foster Wheeler was taken over by Trenergy in 1998-99.

WILLIAMS GROCER, 1962
105 Queenston St. • Built: *c*.1875 (demolished)

When Williams Grocer closed in 1961 it was possibly St. Catharines' oldest store. It was established by John Williams and his wife around 1875. The store was originally a meat and produce market, but after the death of the Williamses, the store was turned into a novelty and variety store by their daughter, Emma, and her husband, Harry Petrie. The store closed in 1961 after Harry died and Emma chose to not manage it on her own. The Williams' store was demolished and has been replaced by the Delta Medical Arts building.

MILLIGAN'S STORE, *c*.1913
135 Queenston St. (cor. of Haynes Ave.)

This grocery business was operated for about a year by Capt. Cecil W. Milligan, a Great Lakes mariner who after this venture owned a smoke shop and billiard hall on St. Paul Street. Seen here is the delivery wagon for Capt. Milligan's grocery. The business was sold to one of his employees, William Welstead Walker, who with his brother-in-law established Roddy & Walker, Grocers in the same building, *c*.1914-19. By the 1970s, the building was occupied by the Crystal Coffee Shop and a fish and chips restaurant. Since 1978, it has been part of Fortis' Family Restaurant.

CITY GAS WORKS, *c.*1900
n.s. Second Canal (s. of Calvin St.) • Built: 1854-55 (demolished)

Founded in 1853 by William Hamilton Merritt Jr., John L. Ranney, James Rae Benson, William A. Chisholm, and Edward Glackmeyer, the St. Catharines and Welland Canal Gas Light Co. produced coal gas used in lighting city streets and Second and Third Canal locks. Operations began in 1855. They eventually had about 100 km (60 miles) of gas mains, not only throughout St. Catharines, but as far as Port Dalhousie and Thorold. The coal used in making the gas was imported from the United States. They also sold the by-products of coal tar, oil tar, coke, and ammonia, as well as stoves, mantles, and fixtures. The business ceased operations (between 1918-43) after electricity and natural gas replaced the need to manufacture synthetic gas.

LINCOLN CANNING CO., *c.*1977
203 Carlton St.

The Lincoln Canning Factory was founded in 1929 by Hubert O'Mara and employed thirty workers in its first year of operation. Initially, they canned only tomatoes, but later added asparagus and other vegetables, plus a full line of fruits. Local growers provided 90% of the fruits and vegetables used at the factory and, prior to the Second World War, they exported their "Lincoln Brand" canned goods to Great Britain and elsewhere. The factory ceased operations around 1977. The process area of the cannery was in the two and one-storey frame sections shown here, since demolished. A number of small businesses occupied the balance of the premises until 1999 when it became Coppola's Ristorante, a use carried on until the present (2005).

ST. CATHARINES GROWERS CO-OPERATIVE, c.1950
9B Balfour St. • Built: 1915

This small store sold feed and farm supplies for over thirty years. It variously operated as Archie Miller's Flour and Feed (1917-20), Titterington Co. Ltd. Wholesale Produce (1921-23), G.H. Mitchell Flour and Feed (1923), Harold Rayner Flour and Feed (1925-1938), and St. Catharines Flour and Feed (1939-45). It became the St. Catharines Growers Co-op Feed Mill in 1946 (at the same time an addition was made to the building), and was conducted by Frederick Lewis Collard from about 1947 to 1951. This small operation was a part of Shur-Gain, a feed-packing company that existed throughout Canada. It remained in business until 1964 selling feed and farm supplies to fruit growers. Various small businesses occupied the premises in the years that followed and it is now a commercial-residential combination.

ALEX'S GARAGE, c.1940
78 Pelham Rd.

From 1927-58 Alex Golchuk owned this Pelham Road building. Though originally known simply as "Golchuk's", the garage was renamed "Alex's" to differentiate it from William Golchuk's (possibly a brother or son to Alex?). The other Golchuk's opened nearby on Kent Street in 1935, where members of the Golchuk family also made their home. Between 1959 and 1961, Epp's Service Centre operated at 78 Pelham Road.

J. Wilson Blacksmith Shop (Homer), 1904
Queenston Rd. (w. of #49) • (demolished)

Known also as the "Upper Ten," the sleepy hamlet of Homer stretched about a mile along both sides of the Queenston Road. It was given the classical name of Homer in 1859, with the establishment of a post office. The village smithy was an important fixture in every community a century ago, sought out to shoe horses, fix wagon wheels, or fashion metalwork over anvil and forge. It was no different in the village of Homer where J. Wilson operated his blacksmith forge. Other smithies in Homer included Jerry Stocking and William E. Cratt.

DeCew Falls Generating Station, c.1911
Power Glen • Built: 1897-98/1904-05 • Builder: Messrs. Angus McDonald & Co. (Thorold) (1898)

Referred to as "The Cradle of Canadian Hydro Electric Industry", the plant at DeCew made history in 1898 when it began the long-distance transmission of electricity to Hamilton, 56.3 km (35 miles) away. It was built by Messrs. Angus McDonald of Thorold and was once considered the most economical plant on the continent. Additional generating units were put into service in 1900, 1905, 1908, and 1912 (by then, the building housing the Power House had been enlarged twice, one of those enlargements is underway in the photo). In October 1943, a new power plant opened just to the east. The plant continues to generate power as part of the Ontario Power Generation system.

Grandstand – Garden City Raceway, 1984
Coon Road (betw. South Service Rd. and Glendale Ave.)
Architect: Earl C. Morgan (Toronto) • (demolished)

Although St. Catharines has a history of harness racing that dates back to the mid-1800s, it was not until 1964 that it was officially introduced to the local raceway. The track was part of the Ontario Jockey Club's rotating circuit, which also included Greenwood Raceway in Toronto and Mohawk Raceway in Campbellville. In the off-season, the track was used for the Kiwanis Horse Show, one of Canada's largest in the variety of classes offered. Garden City Raceway was closed in 1976. Vestiges of the former track survived for a number of years – the spectator seats were used until 1998 in the grandstand overlooking the famous Henley Rowing Course.

Morningstar Mill, 1967
2716 DeCew Rd. • Built: 1872 • Builder: Robert Chappel (Thorold) • Designated: 1997

Morningstar Mill was built from stone quarried from the pond in the foreground of this photograph. The Mill was purchased by the City of St. Catharines in 1875 when it was decided to build a new water reservoir in the area. In 1883, the City sold the mill to Wilson Morningstar and his brother Wallace, who produced flour and horse feed. It was destroyed by fire in 1895, and repaired by the Morningstar brothers. The Mill operated until 1933 when Wilson Morningstar died. It was sold to Ontario Hydro in 1941 at the time of enlargements to their nearby generating facilities. It was then leased to the City of St. Catharines and opened as the Mountain Mills Museum in 1962. The City re-acquired the site in 1989. In the early 1990s, a complete restoration of the dam, roller mill, and turbine shed was completed by Friends of Morningstar Mill. In May 1995, the Mill was again in full working condition.

General Motors Plant 2, 1965
570 Glendale Ave. • Built: 1952 • Architect: Thomas H. Wiley (StC) • Builder: Newman Bros. (StC)

In 1950, General Motors purchased 57 hectares (141 acres) of land on Glendale Avenue to construct a new foundry. When it opened in 1952, the foundry was the largest and most modern malleable and grey iron foundry in the Commonwealth. One year after its official opening, plans were announced to build an Engine Plant at the same site (completed 1954). The new plant produced V-8 Rocket engines for Chevrolet, Pontiac, and Oldsmobile automobiles. The Administration Building for the Glendale Plant was completed in 1965 (demolished 2002). The foundry was closed at the end of 1995, and from 1998 to 2000, a $400 million investment converted the former foundry space into a new line for the manufacture of the leading-edge GEN III engine.

Hayes Steel, 1948
55 Oakdale Ave. (w. of Hickory St.)

Canada Wheel Works was founded in 1865, renamed afterwards as the Pioneer Pole and Shaft, then the Canada Pole and Shaft, and then Hayes Wheels and Forgings Ltd. In 1937, after dropping the wheel business to become an auto parts maker, their name was again changed, this time to Hayes Steel Products Ltd. In 1966, Hayes-Dana Ltd. was formed, capitalizing on the U.S.-Canada Automotive Trade Pact, with divisions established in St. Catharines and Thorold. About 1990 it became home to Niagara Recycling. The forge has been demolished and the section seen above is all that remains of a historic and once large industrial complex in Merritton.

WILLSON CARBIDE WORKS, 1896
Oakdale Ave. (e. of Lock 10, Second Canal, w. of Clark St.) • (demolished)

The Willson Carbide Works was founded by Thomas L. Willson, "The Father of Canada's Electro-Chemical Industry" and inventor of the process to economically produce acetylene gas. Acetylene was used to power streetlights, navigation buoys, headlights, and carriage lamps, and Willson sold his patent to firms in the United States, Canada, and Britain. The Merritton location east of Lock 9 of the Second Canal had the advantage of abundant water and hydroelectric power needed in the manufacturing process. When it began operations on April 13, 1896, it was the first carbide plant in Canada. It was destroyed by fire on April 24, 1914, and rebuilt, but after the death of Thomas Willson a year later, the plant was sold to Shawinigan Chemical. Operations continued locally until 1966.

PHELPS MILL, *c.*1877
at Lock 8, Second Canal (bet. Oakdale Ave. and Moffatt St., w. of Phelps St.) • Built: *c.*1854-55 (destroyed by fire)

The sawmill located at Lock 8, west of Oakdale Avenue opposite Phelps Street, was owned by Noah and Orson Phelps. Built around 1854-55, the Mill was constructed with wood board-and-batten siding. Noah also established the Lincoln Paper Mill in 1877 and was its president until retiring in 1893 due to ill health. He was a man of large stature, standing 193 cm (6'4") and weighing 108.9 kg (240 lbs). About 1873 he lost his forearm in an accident at the mill when it got caught in a planing machine. The mill burned down in 1882, and problems with embezzlement by a family member caused the Phelps' Mill firm to dissolve three years later. Orson Phelps moved on to found the village of Phelpston (Simcoe County), where he lived until 1870 (when he moved to Florence in Lambton County for two years). He then returned to Phelpston where he became Reeve until 1885, the Legislative representative for Simcoe County from 1884 to 1890, and Sheriff of Simcoe County in 1890. He died in Merritton in 1897. Meanwhile, his brother, Noah, was active with Grimsby Park, a Methodist Campground on the shores of Lake Ontario. Noah died in 1900.

ALLIANCE-LINCOLN SULPHITE MILL, *c.*1975
e. of Clark St. (formerly Abbey Ave.) • (demolished *c.*2004) • Built: 1878-79 (demolished c. 2004)

The Lincoln Paper Mills Limited was just one of several paper mills which operated in the St. Catharines-Merritton-Thorold area. The mill was organized in 1877 by Noah A. Phelps with a number of prominent local men as directors: John Conlon, Samuel D. Woodruff, Daniel Moore, Patrick Larkin and Sylvester Neelon. The Sulphite Mill produced highly refined, bleached pulp, which was processed at the adjoining Lincoln Mill into tag stock, insulating paper, heavyweight food packaging and business papers. About 1888, they purchased the MacDonald & Jones paper mill at Lock 7 on the canal (afterwards referred to as "the Lower Lincoln"), and in 1904 acquired the old Lybster cotton mill near today's Glendale Avenue and converted it in 1911 to paper making. The old Lincoln building was heavily damaged in the Merritton Tornado of 1898 when its roof was torn off and its red limestone walls partially destroyed.

DOMTAR PAPER MILL, *c.*1980
w. of Hartzell Rd. and e. of Clark St. (formerly Abbey Ave.) • Built: c. 1917-18 (demolished 2003; October 1984 (main building and possibly sulphite tower)

The big digester building and sulphite acid tower of the Lincoln Mills were constructed about 1918. In 1928 the Lincoln Pulp & Paper Company joined with two other paper makers to form Alliance Paper Mills Limited. Alliance was one of the largest employers in the area with over 500 workers. Domtar Pulp & Paper Limited purchased Alliance Paper Mills Limited in 1962. Pulpwood was used for making paper and a familiar sight on the property was a 'mountain' of logs awaiting processing. The Sulphite Pulp Mill and Lincoln Board Mill were shut down on January 31, 1968 and Domtar ceased all St. Catharines operations in 2002. The buildings have been demolished and the former Lincoln-Alliance site, including the original Lincoln mill, is part of the brownfield development underway in 2005 by the Merritton Mills Redevelopment Corporation.

INDEPENDENT RUBBER CO., *c*.1912-19
344 Glendale Ave. • Built: 1882-83 (destroyed by fire 1961)

When an earlier building at 344 Glendale opened in 1857, it was known as the Beaver Cotton Mills. It remained a cotton mill for 49 years, during which period it became the Merritton Cotton Mills Co. The frame building was destroyed by fire in 1881 and was rebuilt in Grimsby formation stone. It was not until 1912 that the Independent Rubber Company occupied the premises to produce rubber footwear. It remained open until 1919, when competition with the Consolidated Rubber Company in Port Dalhousie caused Independent's closure. From 1935, the building was used for storage by the Interlake Tissue Mill. The main east building (pictured) was destroyed in a spectacular fire on May 21, 1961. The smaller building in the industrial complex (not visible in the photo) was then used by Domtar for storage. In 2001, the building was sold to the Merritton Development Inc. who have completely renovated and restored the historic structure. It has been home to The Keg restaurant since November 8, 2002.

ALLIANCE EMPLOYEES CREDIT UNION, *c*.1977
344 Glendale Ave. (w. of Merritt St.) • Built: *c*.1883 (demolished 1980)

The Independent Rubber Co. owned several smaller buildings around its main plant. This one served as the office for the footwear manufacturer, adapted years later as the credit union of the Alliance Paper Company employees. The rubber works also had other buildings to board its workers. The former office/credit union building was demolished in 1980 to make way for the realignment of Glendale Avenue just to the south. In 2006 the road will be returned to the vicinity of its original location as part of plans by the Region to improve the Glendale-Merritt intersection.

MERRITTON LIONS CLUB MEMORIAL SWIMMING POOL, 1949
40 Seymour Ave. (cor. Park) • Built: 1948 (swimming pool and wading pool); 1949 (bath house) • Builder: Rymer Bros.

The Merritton Lions Club, founded in 1939, undertook a fundraising campaign for a public swimming pool. Their goal was to prevent children from swimming in the Canal, a pastime that sometimes resulted in tragic deaths. By 1948, the Club had raised $30,000 and the pool project was able to proceed. It opened on July 17, 1949 under manager Bob Dunn. It was named the Merritton Lions Club Memorial Swimming Pool in honour of the area's war veterans. The original free pool was removed in the mid-1990s owing to maintenance problems and replaced with a new city-owned pool with an admission charge. It was renamed c.2003 the Lion Dunc Schooley Pool after the long-time Lions Club member.

MERRITTON WATERWORKS, c.1927
s.s. Beaverdams Road (w. of WSC) • Built: 1927 • (demolished 1993)

This waterworks plant, though located in Thorold where water was available, solely serviced the village of Merritton. The system for drawing water was laid by Garson & Purcer of St. Catharines in 1887, updated in 1927, and enlarged in 1955. A hydro system was initiated in 1908, and in 1919, the Water and Hydro departments merged to form the Merritton Public Utilities Commission. Seen in the photo are Superintendent John V. Barber (in doorway), and from left to right, Arthur B. Collins, John Duff, and Ward F. Nice. While the settling pond for the waterworks still exists, the building was declared surplus by the Regional Municipality of Niagara and demolished in 1993.

UNION TAVERN, *c.*1930-40
315 Merritt St. (renumbered in 1950 from #121-123)

Boasting of having "stood with Merritton since its incorporation," Hallett's Coach House on Merritt Street has long been known as simply the "Union Tavern." Dating back to the 1870s, the building was acquired by Robert E. Hallett in the early 1900s. It is said that the tavern provided food and lodging for travellers and immigrant workers during construction of the Welland Canal.

MAIN'S DRUG STORE, *c.*1948
325 Merritt St. (renumbered from #131 in 1950)

A number of druggists have occupied this central Merritton location, including Hugh J. Main. He operated a drug store here from about 1930 until 1967. The store also featured a soda bar, sold stationery, and advertised cigars for sale from its storefront. It has been the Milk Maid Shoppe convenience store since 1968. Up until 1984, the second floor was the meeting hall for Livingston Lodge No. 130, IOOF. This Merritton Oddfellows Lodge was formed prior to the First World War.

W.A. RICHARDSON STORE, *c.*1910
337 Merritt St. (renumbered in 1950 from #139)

In 1907, William A. Richardson bought this grocery store. His son Frank took over in 1945. When the store ceased business in 1968, groceries had been sold from there for about 100 years. In 1973 the building was purchased by Finnegan's Upholstery who used it until 1974. Since 1977, it has been a used appliance store, with Star Appliances occupying the premises from 1984. In the photo above, William stands in front of his store. The young boy on the left is Albert, also referred to as 'Bert' (who died at about age 4-5). Claude is on the right and another son Frank was born later. They lived on the premises, along with William's wife Belle and daughter Edith.

MERRITTON TAVERN, *c.*1949
355 Merritt St. (renumbered in 1950 from #155,157) • Architect: Sidney Rose Badgley (StC)

John Conner first opened the Merritton Tavern in 1878, under the name of The Mansion House, a popular name at the time. The Ricci family bought the tavern in 1928, and converted the building into a boarding house. In 1934, they reconverted it into a tavern (named the Merritton Tavern, seen here), and in 1952 the building was renamed Ricci's Tavern. By the 1990s, the building had become Ego's, and looks much different than the earlier tavern. As of 2005, it provides rental rooms under the name of The Merritt.

Riordon Paper Mill, 1910
219 Merritt St. • Built: 1867 • Architect: William B. Allan (StC) • Builder: Edwin Switzer (StC)

In 1862, John Riordon and his brother Charles leased a property from Thomas R. Merritt to build a wrapping paper mill near Lock 6 on the Second Welland Canal. The first mill was sold in 1874 and became the Whitman and Barnes Manufacturing Company. John Riordon's second mill, a sulphite mill, was opened in Canada's Confederation year near Lock 18 of the Second Welland Canal. Riordon, the "Father of the Canadian Pulp and Paper Industry," introduced paper derived from wood pulp, as opposed to cloth or straw. The mill supplied paper to many newspapers, including *The Globe* (Toronto) and *The Mail* (Toronto), which in 1895 Riordon merged into *The Mail & Empire*, the *Weekly Telegraph and Sun* (St. John, N.B.), the *Montreal Witness*, the Hamilton *Spectator*, the Quebec *Chronicle*, the Buffalo *Courier*, etc. The mill operated until 1920 when it was forced to close due to a depression in the paper industry. The International Paper Company bought it five years later, but it was again abandoned. Parts of the building, built of Grimsby formation stone are still visible from Merritt Street, surrounded by later additions and occupied by Sun Collision.

McCleary and McLean Planing Mills, c.1890
Merritt St. (adjacent to the Second Canal near Locks 17 to 21) • Built: late-1840s (demolished c. 1911)

The McCleary and McLean Lumber and Planing Mills were near the Thorold-Merritton town line on the Second Canal, a location which was a source of abundant water needed to power their mills. The mills produced fine lumber, flooring, siding, and shingles. The upper story of the planing mill turned out builders' materials, such as door and window frames made of pine and oak, the mill's specialty woods. They did an active trade with shipbuilders and were also responsible for the Canal's timber contracts from 1876 until at least 1906. It is believed that the mills were demolished about 1911 and replaced by the Kimberly-Clark paper mill.

THE WOOD HOUSE, c.1877-84
38 Lakeport Rd. (formerly Front St.) • Built: 1877 (destroyed by fire 1884)

Before it burned in the 1870s, the canal-side building at Lock 1 of the Second Canal was occupied by the Thompson Hotel, Denton's Tailor Shop, and John Wood's Grocery store. It was replaced by a new building in 1877 which was built by Richard Wood, and became known as the Wood House Hotel. The building again burned in 1884, and was replaced by Edward Murphy with a new brick structure. The building's situation along the Canal was convenient to serving sailors and their vessels, like the tugboat *AUGUSTA* in Lock 1 of the Second Welland Canal.

MURPHY AND SCOTT'S SHIP CHANDLERY, c.1910-13
38 Lakeport Rd. (formerly Front St.) • Built: 1885 • Designated 1980, De-designated 2003

In 1885, Edward Murphy established a popular ship chandlery in this two-storey, red-brick building at the corner of Lock Street. It was rebuilt on the same site as one destroyed by fire the previous year. Murphy started in the business about 1878 and was joined by a partner, Frank Scott, in 1891. On the first floor they retailed food and supplies to local residents and to docked seamen, while the second floor held a sort of "lounge" for sportsmen, politicians, and press people. In 1950, the building was sold to former employee Bill Latcham. He owned the business until 1976 when Dr. Blake Harley undertook renovations to the historic structure. Murphy's Restaurant became a fixture at the site in 1978. The men in the photo are, from left, Wilfred Murphy, Frank Scott, Henry Scott, Dick Taylor, Edward Murphy, and an unknown 'traveller' (salesman).

FIRST RUBBER WORKS, *c.*1895
63 Lakeport Rd. • Built: 1850 (destroyed by fire 1899)

The R. & J. Lawrie Flouring and Grist Mills opened in 1850, built and operated by John Lawrie, who was also the first Reeve of the Village of Port Dalhousie (1862), and Robert Lawrie, Deputy Reeve for St. Catharines (1870). The mill was sold to Norris and Neelon of St. Catharines, who operated it as the Ontario Mills. Discussions were underway as early as 1885 about using "Capt. Neelon's mill" for a rubber factory. It is believed that in 1890, it was taken over by the Toronto Rubber Co. (later referred to as Maple Leaf Rubber). On January 2, 1899, the building was destroyed in a catastrophic fire that put 250 workers out of a job. A mammoth two-building brick complex was constructed on the site and opened in 1900.

Maple Leaf Rubber Co., c.1905
62-63 Lakeport Rd. • Built: 1899-1900 (warehouse annex demolished c.1966) • Builder: George Wilson & Co. Planing Mill & Box Factory (StC)

In 1900, two new buildings for the Maple Leaf Rubber Co. were completed to replace the earlier ones destroyed by fire. Situated on opposite sides of Lakeport Road between Martindale Pond and the inner harbour, the main five-storey building boasted a mansard-roofed tower and an additional floor level that was below the grade of the road, all of which was connected to the four-storey warehouse opposite by means of an overhead skywalk. It joined the fourth floor of the main building to the third of the annex. A 1907 account of their "Maple Leaf" and "Toronto" brands of rubber footwear boasted "These goods are to be found in the stores of every town and city of the Dominion of Canada." Maple Leaf Rubber operated until 1907 when it was taken over by Consolidated Rubber. In 1927 the factory closed altogether. Various smaller companies then used the building until 1955. Lincoln Fabrics then occupied the building and continues there today in the manufacture of industrial fabrics. The four-storey warehouse on the west side of the road, part of this two-building complex, was demolished about 1966.

PORT DALHOUSIE POST OFFICE AND GROCERY STORE, *c*.1905
12, 14 Lock St. • Built: *c*.1896

A post office in Port Dalhousie was first opened in 1832 under Postmaster George Smith. Postmasters who followed included: Nathan Pawling, John H. Martindale, Richard Wood, Johnson I. Gregory, Eugene F. Dwyer, and A. Kelly. In 1837, mail was delivered by horseback twice weekly from St. Catharines. The post office was in the Wood House when it burned in 1884. James Stanton, Postmaster from 1895 until 1925, purchased this lot on Lock Street in 1896 and it is believed built this building about that time. Stanton's "Fine Groceries" (*l*) stocked fancy and staple goods, canned stuffs, and family supplies. An ice cream parlour and Post Office (*r*) is advertised on the right side of the building. Stanton died in 1925 and his family continued to own the building until 1973. It has since been host to a variety of retail, craft, and restaurant operations. After Stanton's service as Postmaster, the position was filled by Wilfred Laurier Hart, and then Robert Francis Gamble. In 1962, the Port Dalhousie Post Office, by then located on Main Street, was closed and re-assigned to P.O. #2 at St. Catharines.

SCOTT'S ICE HOUSE, c.1914-15
location unknown • (demolished)

By the 1940s, refrigerators began to replace the icebox and blocks of ice as the preferred means of keeping food cool. Prior to that, ice would be harvested in large blocks from Martindale Pond. Ice crews would regularly clean snow from the pond to keep the ice from softening. When the pond had frozen at least a foot, crews would use pike poles and grids to mark the location and size of the ice to be cut. The ice would be cut with wide-toothed ice saws, pulled out with ice tongs, and loaded onto a sleigh that would be pulled by horse to one of at least three icehouses in Port Dalhousie. Ice would then be delivered door to door for use in residential iceboxes while the town's children ran behind the delivery wagon in the hope of picking up errant pieces of the refreshing ice. A billboard in the lower right of the photo advertises "Mason & Risch Pianos," available at their branch factory stores in St. Catharines and Niagara Falls.

LAKESIDE PARK ADMINISTRATION BUILDING, *c.*1925
Lakeside Park • Built: *c.*1922 (demolished)

Lakeside Park was developed shortly after the NS&T completed their Port Dalhousie line in 1901. The Park was doubled in size in 1922 when additional land was purchased. Some of the Park's attractions included a water slide (removed in 1950 for safety reasons), bumper cars, paddle boats, and the famous Merry-go-Round. The midway, excepting the Merry-go-Round, was dismantled in 1970. The dance pavilion burned in 1974.

PORT DALHOUSIE CANNING COMPANY, *c.*1913
201 Main St. • Built: 1913

Located on the NS&T Railway Port Dalhousie line, the Port Dalhousie Canning Company was opened in 1913 by Chris Fretz of Vineland. They packaged an average of 50,000 cases of fruits and vegetables each year. The company was taken over by Canadian Canners in 1923, the biggest canning company in the country, and they shifted processing and packing operations to other area canners. Thereafter, the Port Dalhousie building was used only for storage. It was last listed in city directories in 1927. The Lions Club purchased the old cannery for a community centre in June 1952. The Port Dalhousie Scouts use the second floor for meetings.

Six
Education

ST. CATHARINES BOARD OF EDUCATION, 1936
15 Welland Ave. • Built: 1865 • Builder: John Clyde (StC)

The Board of Education building was originally built as a home for bank manager George W. Pierce. It was designed in the Second Empire style. In 1904, Pierce moved out and Ralph B. Hamilton occupied the building (until 1917). The Board of Education moved into the building in 1919. It was originally intended as a residence for the teachers at Memorial School, but costs for such a plan were too high. It was then used until the 1960s as the Board's Administration Offices. The Board of Education moved to 112 Oakdale Avenue about 1962 (and to a new Board office at 191 Carlton Street in 1991). From 1963 until 1964, Brock University used the Welland Avenue building for their Administration Offices when the University was being established. The building at 15 Welland Avenue became a restaurant for a brief period of time before Picasso's Hair Salon acquired it. This official-looking group at the Welland Avenue offices of the St. Catharines Board of Education is possibly the Board's elected Trustees and administrators. Only one woman – Estelle Cuffe Hawley – punctuates the male-dominated profession. Not only a trailblazer in education, she also broke new ground for women in politics, social welfare, and health care.
Pictured in the photo are: Back row (l to r): Dr. A.R. Lindsay, Miss Estelle B. Cuffe, W. Percy Holmes, Dr. W.H. Cunningham, A.H. Trapnell, G.a. Robertson (Lincoln County rep.), W.J. Salter (Collegiate Principal) [far right]. Front row (l to r): Percy M. Hulse, F.J. Flynn (Separate School rep.), F.E. Hetherington, F.R. Paxton (Lincoln County rep.), A.A. Craise (Lincoln County rep.), Dr. J.M. Shutis, Chairman, W.H. Irvine, C.T. McBride, Secretary-Treasurer.

GRANTHAM ACADEMY, 1866
85 Church St. (renumbered from #89) • Built: 1829 • Designated 1978

This Church Street school has undergone a number of changes and additions since its establishment. When opened in 1829, it was known as the Grantham Academy and was the second grammar school in Ontario. In 1845, when St. Catharines was incorporated as a town, the school was renamed the St. Catharines & District Grammar School. It remained a grammar school until the School Act was passed in 1871. In 1872 it became the St. Catharines Collegiate Institute. A.E. 'Scout' Coombs was the popular Principal of the old Collegiate from 1909 until its closing in 1923 when the school relocated to the new classic-designed edifice at 34 Catherine Street. The old school then became the W.J. Robertson Public School, named for a local principal who was one of Canada's foremost scholars and textbook authors. The school was renovated in 1952 after the interior was ravaged by fire. It closed in 1977 due to low enrolment and since 1985 has been home to the Folk Arts Council Multicultural Centre.

St. Catharines Collegiate Institute and Vocational School, c.1923
34 Catherine St. • Built: 1922-23/1949/1963 • Architect: S.B. Coon & Son (Toronto) • Builder: W.H. Yates Construction (Hamilton)

Shortly after the First World War, the old Grantham Academy on Church Street, by then renamed the St. Catharines Collegiate, had become outdated and overcrowded. A petition for a new high school in the city went unheeded for many years because of a funding shortfall (particularly owing to the construction of the new bridge to west St. Catharines). Various sites were considered and finally, in 1922, construction for the school was begun. The new Collegiate opened in September of the following year (though the official dedication did not take place until November 5th). The new school was far bigger than the old, with an auditorium that seated 900. It also contained several labs, a library, and a shop wing, all of which the old Grantham Academy building lacked. The six magnificent Doric columns on the front façade give the St. Catharines Collegiate a classical appearance.

RIDLEY COLLEGE (SPRINGBANK HOTEL), c.1891
Yates St. (e.s. at College, about #68 Yates St.) • Built: 1864 (destroyed by fire 1903)

The Springbank Sanatorium on Yates Street was advertised for sale after the death of its founder, Dr. Theophilus Mack, in 1881. In November 1888, Bishop Ridley College was founded and named after Nicholas Ridley, a 16th century Bishop of London. The founders were low-church Anglicans from St. Catharines and Toronto who wanted a private low-church boarding school to prepare their sons for entrance to the evangelical Wycliffe College at the University of Toronto. An organizing meeting in September 1888 was quickly followed with a founding meeting in November. The School's first students arrived in September 1889. The school remained in the old spa building, seen above, until it was destroyed by fire on October 25, 1903.

RIDLEY COLLEGE, c.1913
2 Ridley Rd.

After a disastrous fire in 1903 at the former Springbank building, Ridley College began rebuilding at their present Ridley Road location on the west side of Twelve Mile Creek. The Upper, or Senior School, was built in 1904 and officially opened in 1905. The Lower, or Junior School, built in 1899 (and replaced in 1927), differed greatly in appearance, being built in the early-Georgian style. The Dean's residential house was built in 1908 in the Tudor style. Other buildings in the photo include the gymnasium, built in 1910, and the rink, built in 1902 (but destroyed by fire in 1918). Campus facilities have expanded significantly in the century since this photo.

T.D. PHILLIPS PRIVATE SCHOOL, 1863
92 Henry St. (formerly at 18 Elm St., and originally on Academy St.) • Built: 1853 • Builder: James Dougan, Sr. (StC) • Designated: 2004

Rev. Thomas D. Phillips taught at the Grantham Academy in the early 1860s, but was dismissed, and established his own school in a one-storey house on Academy Street, where this photo was taken. Though Phillips left the school in 1866 to establish a second school in Ottawa, the St. Catharines school continued to bear his name. In 1911, the building was moved to 18 Elm (now Hetherington) Street, until the early 1920s, when the new St. Catharines Collegiate required the land there. The Phillips Private School moved its building again to nearby Henry Street. Throughout its many moves, the building retained its original beams and gable roof. The building continues to stand at 92 Henry Street.

St. Thomas' / St. Andrew's Ward School, c.1959
13-15 Church St. • Built: 1853 (demolished 1961)

The school at the corner of Church and William Streets was originally named the St. Thomas' Ward School, but was renamed when the wards were restructured. The school closed in 1954 due to low enrolment, and the students were sent to Memorial School on Welland Avenue. It was briefly reopened in 1955 for the students of Central School, whose building had been condemned. It afterwards operated as the St. Catharines Emergency Measures Organization, until it was razed in 1961 and replaced with a modern office tower, home to Provincial Gas from 1967 (later Enbridge Gas).

St. Paul's Ward School, c.1940s
227 Church St. • Built: 1872 (demolished 1950)

This Victorian-style school was replaced in 1951, with a modern structure housing Loblaw's Grocery Store. The store remained there until 1971, and from 1973 to 1983 became the Regional Municipality of Niagara Public Works offices and the Niagara Land Division offices. Since 1983 it has been home to Delta Bingo.

ST. GEORGE'S WARD SCHOOL/CENTRAL PUBLIC SCHOOL (ST. CATHARINES), 1940S
143 Church St. • Built: 1853 (demolished 1955)

This red-brick schoolhouse on Church Street was known as St. George's Ward School until 1872 when it was significantly enlarged and renamed Central Public School. In the winter of 1954 the school was condemned as unsafe. E.I. McCulley was Principal at the time. Its students were sent to the old St. Andrew's Ward School, Memorial School, and Robertson School until permanent schools could be found. Central was demolished in 1955 and the following year the present St. Nicholas Catholic School was erected in its place (the original St. Nicholas was built next door in 1857, replaced by a two-storey brick structure in 1887 [seen here to the right], and demolished in 1967 to make way for École Immaculée-Conception).

COURT STREET SCHOOL, c.1959
e.s. Court St. at 23 Centre St. • Built: 1890-91 • Builder: Newman Bros. (StC)

Originally known as the St. George's Ward Primary School, this four-room school was re-named the Court Street School in 1927. By 1900, ten years after its opening, the school had hot water and could accommodate 240 children. The school was closed in 1952 and the Masonic Memorial Temple purchased the building. The Niagara Conservatory of Music shares the building with the Masons.

VICTORIA PUBLIC SCHOOL, *c*.1911
173 Niagara St. • Built: 1911-12/1929 • Architect: Thomas H. Wiley (StC) (1912/1929) • Builder: Newman Bros. (StC)

On March 17, 1910, the Board of Education authorized the purchase of land for a new school on Niagara Street. Built at a cost of $30,500, the two-storey, eight-room school was ready for classes in September 1912. The red-brick school was also the first in St. Catharines to provide a separate entrance for the kindergarten so as to not disrupt older students during early dismissal. An additional 22.9 m (75′) of land was purchased in 1928 for the 1929 construction of a four-room addition at the northeast corner of the building.

VICTORIA PUBLIC SCHOOL, c.1950
173 Niagara St. • Built: 1911-12/1929 • Architect: Thomas H. Wiley (StC) • Builder: Newman Bros. (StC)

Victoria Public School celebrated its Diamond Jubilee in June 1972. A special address was given by Ashton Morrison who was head of the school for 28 years from 1925 until 1953. In 1983, Victoria School was used as the venue, and many of its pupils were hired as extras, for the filming of the holiday classic, *A Christmas Story*. Declining enrolments forced the closure of the school at the end of the 2001 school year. It was purchased three years later by Women's Place of St. Catharines & North Niagara for an expanded thirty-bedroom shelter. The former playground was sold and will be subdivided into a combination of single-family units and townhouses under a separate development plan scheduled to commence in 2006.

ALEXANDRA PUBLIC SCHOOL, 1909
84 Henry St. • Built: 1909 • Architect: Stewart and Whitton (Hamilton) • Builder: Newman Bros. (StC)

Ten years before Alexandra School was built, the School Board was aware of the need for another school in the Dufferin Street area to replace the old St. Patrick's Ward School, but the cost of property was not affordable at the time. Eventually, the entire block surrounded by Henry, Dufferin, Pleasant, and George Streets, was purchased for the construction of the school. In December 1909, Alexandra School was officially opened with Miss M. Holmes as headmistress. At the time, Alexandra was the largest public school in the city. J.S. Elliott was a popular principal closely identified with the school. Under Mr. Elliott, Alexandra and Victoria always enjoyed a healthy rivalry in sporting competitions. The school underwent a major renovation in 1998.

Connaught Public School, 1959
28 Prince St. • Built: 1915 • Architect: Thomas H. Wiley (StC) • Builder: Newman Bros. (StC)

In 1915, Prince Arthur, the Duke of Connaught and the tenth Governor General of Canada, visited St. Catharines. The elementary school on Prince Street was under construction at the time, and was named after him. The two-and-a-half storey building is similar in appearance to Victoria School on Niagara Street, also designed by T.H. Wiley and constructed by Newman Bros. The original eight-classroom school was enlarged in the 1940s and again in 1964 when the gymnasium was added. It underwent a $1.75 million upgrade in 2002-2003. One of its more famous former pupils was Leonard Birchall, "The Saviour of Ceylon." Highly decorated for his heroic actions during the Second World War, Birchall returned to his community in October 1945. His former school planted a tree in his honour.

MEMORIAL PUBLIC SCHOOL, 1959
17 Welland Ave. • Built: 1919-20

Memorial School was built in response to a population boom in St. Catharines. The building's modern, one-floor design was exceptionally different from the previous two-storey St. Catharines schools. There were several small houses on the grounds, used briefly as teachers' residences, and an adjacent larger brick house that held the Board's administration offices. The school was also unique in that it was the first to be equipped with telephones during the building process. The School's first principal was Frank Mittlefehldt. Among the student population were children from the nearby Protestant Orphans Home on Ontario Street. The school was enlarged in 1928, and underwent further renovations in 2000. Until these alterations and additions, Memorial had a twin in west St. Catharines. Named after the World War I nurse/heroine, Edith Cavell School was built to the same design at approximately the same time.

GLENRIDGE PUBLIC SCHOOL, c.1959
101 South Dr. (formerly Ontario St. S.) • Built: 1929/1953 • Architect: Nicholson & Macbeth (StC) (1929) (StC) / Wilson A. Salter (StC) (1953) • Builder: Newman Bros. (StC) (1929)

This school, with its slate roof, leaded glass casement windows and stone-trimmed cinder brick walls, was architects Nicholson and Macbeth's solution for an institutional building designed to match to their similarly-detailed residences in the well-to-do new Glenridge subdivision. When the school opened in 1929, only two of the four classrooms were used. In 1953, architect Wilson A. Salter added an Assembly Hall (later used as the library), and four additional classrooms. A gymnasium was added in 1989, and further renovations in 1999 were made to the heating, plumbing, and electrical systems. The first principal of Glenridge Public School was Miss Dorothy Moote.

QUEEN ELIZABETH WARTIME EMERGENCY SCHOOL, c.1959
1 Currie St. (at Dieppe Rd.) • Built: 1943

This four-room school was opened in 1943, funded by the Wartime Housing Corporation. During the Second World War, emergency housing communities, such as the one in the QEW-Niagara Street area, were established to provide temporary homes for factory workers and their families, all in support of the war effort. Fred McQuiggin was the school's first Principal. Queen Elizabeth was last used as a public school in 1962. The building was vacant until about 1968 when Sts. Cyril and Methodius Church opened a Ukrainian Catholic Separate School. Kids Place Child Care Centre has occupied the premises since May of 2000.

SIR WINSTON CHURCHILL SCHOOL, c.1959
201 Glenridge Ave. • Built: 1955 • Architect: Lionel A. Hesson (StC) • Builder: Rymer Bros. (StC)

In 1955, during the last year of his second term as Prime Minister, Sir Winston Churchill wrote to the St. Catharines School Board granting them permission to name their newly-built elementary school on Glenridge Avenue after him. Ernest I. McCulley was the school's first Principal. In 1959, the school was converted into a secondary school. By this time Oakridge Public School had just opened on Marsdale Drive and the St. Catharines Collegiate high school was becoming overcrowded. A new purpose-built secondary school was constructed on Glen Morris Drive and Sir Winston Churchill relocated there in 1964. The school then reverted to an elementary school (Lady Spencer Churchill School), and from 1994 until 2003 it would be used for the Board's special needs students as the Churchill Learning Centre. The school closed about 2003 and was sold to the Southridge Community Church who offered their first service in the renovated building on December 14, 2003. They also provide an extension ministry shelter for the community.

BRIARDALE PUBLIC SCHOOL, 1958
1A Caroline St. • Built: 1958 • Architect: Wilson A. Salter (StC) • Builder: Daniel W. Holmes (Thorold)

In 1957, the St. Catharines Board of Education purchased 2.4 hectares (6 acres) of land from Oscar F. Jacobson of Merritton for $7,800 for construction of Briardale Elementary School. The name was chosen via a contest run by the Board, and suggested by Colleen Glass, one of the first students of the school. The first principal was Ralph G. VanDusen.

NORTH WARD PUBLIC SCHOOL, pre-1898

Smythe St. • Built: 1875 (demolished c.1943) • Builder: Drysdale and Kirby (StC)

The roof of this small one-room brick schoolhouse was torn off by the Merritton Tornado of 1898. Unfortunately, one student died in the disaster, though it would have been much worse were it not for the quick response of Miss Ida Smyth who came to the aid of her 32 students. The grateful townspeople awarded her a special medal in appreciation.

VALLEY WOOD PUBLIC SCHOOL, c.1962

6½ A Smythe St. • Built: 1942-43/1949 • Architect: William M. Wilson (StC) (1943) • Builder: J.R. Stork & Son (StC) (1943)

In 1942, the former North Ward Public School on Smythe Street had grown too small to house all of the children in this area of Merritton. This newer, two-room school was built on the same street, and the old school acted as an emergency one-room annex. The new school was called the Smythe Street School, until 1962, when the name was changed to Valley Wood Public School. An addition of four rooms was made to the building in 1949. Enrolment peaked in 1977, but within seven years the school's population had dwindled to only 55 students. It was forced to close. The building has been converted into apartments.

Central Public School, Merritton, Canada

CENTRAL PUBLIC SCHOOL (MERRITTON), *c.*1910
361 Glendale Ave. (formerly Concession Rd.) • Built: 1893 (demolished 1979) • Architect: Samuel G. Dolson (StC)
Builder: Newman Bros. (StC)

Merritton's Central Public School was built in the typical style of the late-19th century. The two-storey school had six rooms, separate entrances for male and female students, and was made of red brick with an open belfry attached to the roof. William Jameson was appointed the first principal at an annual salary of $600. In 1920, a kindergarten school was built across the road as an annex to Central Public School. It was later named Glen Merritt School and Central became Glen Merritt Jr. Public School. It was demolished after providing 86 years of education to Merrittonians.

PORT DALHOUSIE PUBLIC SCHOOL, *c.*1910
70 Main St. • Built: 1877 (demolished 1988)

Port Dalhousie Public School served the residents of Port Dalhousie for 102 years, until 1979, before it closed and converted into a family-owned antique market. The original three-classroom school was designed in the Italianate style and included an impressive bell tower. In 1913, a second floor was added, and, in 1948, a further addition was made to the rear of the building. In 1955, the building was renamed "McArthur School", in honour of George A. McArthur who was principal from 1938 until 1947. In 1988 the old school was demolished to make way for the Bayside Village condominium complex.

St. Joseph's Convent, c.1970
63 Church St. • Built: 1874 (destroyed by fire in 1972 and demolished in 1973)

The Sisters of St. Joseph's Academy came from Toronto in 1856 to teach in the new St. Catharines Separate School system. Classes commenced in 1857. Accommodation for the Sisters was in a tiny frame house on Church Street. The new convent, depicted here, would not be built until 1874. The impressive three-storey structure, in two colours of brick, contained forty rooms, a chapel, ornate staircases, several fireplaces, and stained glass windows. In addition to being home to the Sisters, it served as a select Academy until around 1897. It afterwards became a private elementary school, and then a private high school for girls. When Denis Morris High School opened in 1958, however, most of the students withdrew from the Convent to attend the new Catholic high school. The Sisters taught at twelve separate schools in the area, but continued living in the convent, next to St. Catherine of Alexandria R.C. Church (whose altar was under their care). The Convent was sold in 1969. It was destroyed by fire on November 2, 1972 and the remains demolished a year later. The Misener building was erected in 1981, now under the ownership of the Algoma Central group.

Seven
Public Buildings

MERRITTON TOWN HALL, 1909
343 Merritt St. • Built: 1879 • Architect: William B. Allan (StC) • Builder: James McDonald (Thorold); John Walker (Thorold) (stonemasonry) • Designated: 1978

In 1877, the Village of Merritton purchased a plot of land from John Riordon as a site for a town hall. The Victorian-style hall was built by James McDonald of Thorold for $3000, with stonemasonry by John Walker. It has undergone many changes in its lifetime. Besides serving as the town's municipal offices, it was used in part as a library until that function moved across the street into the Carnegie Library in 1924. The Fire Department, formed in 1888, used the rear part of the ground floor for a Fire Hall – remnants of which still exist (though most of it was destroyed, then rebuilt, after a major fire on April 23, 1929). The Police also had their offices in the Town Hall, with holding cells in the basement. At various times it has also housed the Red Cross, Civil Defence, Waterworks Commission, Post Office, School Board, and Hydro Commission. It ceased as the Town Hall in 1961 when Merritton was amalgamated with St. Catharines. From 1965 until 1990, it was home to the St. Catharines Historical Museum, opened in 1967. After a complete retrofit, it became the new Merritton Senior Citizens Centre in 1995. The photo above shows some of the townspeople beside a wagon with timbers labelled "1829," possibly from the First Welland Canal. The bandstand to the right is now the site of the Merritton Cenotaph, dedicated in 1921.

Lincoln County Courthouse, *c.*1905
91 King St. • Built: 1848-49, 1863-65 • Architect: Kivas Tully (Toronto) (1849) / John Latshaw (Drummondville/NF) (1865) • Builder: William Barron (StC) (1849) / Samuel G. Dolson (StC) (1865) • Designated: 1978

The Old Courthouse was originally built as a Town Hall and Market House for St. Catharines, opening in 1849. The Hall also housed market stalls, a police lockup, and the town's fire wagon before a central Fire Hall was built. Kivas Tully, a respected Toronto architect who also designed the Courthouse in Welland and Victoria Hall in Cobourg, was instructed to design a finer building than the Town Hall in Niagara. The sweeping stone balustrade leading up to the front doors is one of the building's unique features. In 1863-65, the James Street wing was added to house the Lincoln County and Superior Court offices, while the Town offices, including the newly-moved County offices from Niagara, remained in the original main building. The building continued to serve its County functions until it relocated to a new Courthouse in 1981. One of the old gas-lit chandeliers from the main courtroom is now housed at the new Courthouse, while the other is located at the St. Catharines Museum at Lock 3.

MARKET SQUARE, c.1900
cor. King and James Streets

A public market has existed in St. Catharines since at least the 1820s. Originally located in the St. Paul-Ontario Street area, the Market moved to its present location at about the time of the opening of the Town Hall in 1849. Local residents would buy their produce, eggs, meat, and cheese, while farmers would buy, sell, or trade hay, livestock, wood, and coal. On Saturdays (the busiest market day), the entire downtown bustled with activity as rural inhabitants also took the opportunity while in town to visit doctors, banks, shops, family, and friends. The old police headquarters, formerly the Benson carriage house and stables, are visible at the top right, while the public weigh scales and Market Clerk's office are at the top left of the picture.

PUBLIC WEIGH SCALES, 1952
Market Square • Built: 1888 (demolished May 1954)

The Public Weigh Scales in the Market Square were used to weigh livestock, hay, wood, and produce. The Market Clerk operated the scales and provided official weight receipts to vendors. The Clerk's office was in the same building. Towards the end of their existence, the weigh scales were also used to weigh loads of scrap iron. Rarely used by the 1950s, the building that housed the scales was deemed unsafe and was demolished in 1953.

OLD CITY HALL, c.1910
w.s. James St. (cor. of Church St.) • Built: 1841-42 (demolished 1936) • Builder: Samuel Haight (StC) and William Pay (StC)

This home, originally built for James Clendennan, the village schoolteacher, was later occupied by Senator James Rae Benson, a hardware merchant. He sold it to the City of St. Catharines in 1878 when the municipal offices were moved out of the Town Hall which had been taken over for County functions. The building was used as the City Hall until demolished in 1936 to make way for the present one which opened the following year. The cannons in front were moved to the Armouries on Lake Street and the Watson Monument, which is dedicated to Pvt. Alexander Watson who was killed in the Northwest Rebellion of 1885, was relocated diagonally to face the intersection of Church and James Streets.

CITY HALL, c.1953
50 Church St. • Built: 1937 • Architect: Robert Ian Macbeth (StC) • Builder: W.H. Yates Construction (Hamilton) • Designated 1978

By the 1930s, the former Clendennan/Benson residence, which had been converted for use as the City Hall, was no longer able to adequately accommodate all of the civic departments and records of St. Catharines. Plans for a new City Hall were prepared, to be located near the site of the old, and on August 9, 1937 the present municipal offices were opened officially. The cost of the building was $142,066.21. It embodied design elements of the Art Deco style. The interior features terrazzo floors and stairs, as well as brass doors. The Coat of Arms of the City, as well as the symbols for justice and electricity, are depicted on the front façade, and those for science and knowledge on the James Street façade. An addition was made to the rear of the building in 1981. The big banner in the photo proclaims, *Long Live the Queen*. It is believed to commemorate the 1953 Coronation of Queen Elizabeth II, though it could be for another royal visit such as that for the opening of the St. Lawrence Seaway in 1959.

CITY HALL – CITY CLERK'S OFFICE, 1945

When the new City Hall first opened, all Assessment notices, tax bills, and other records were recorded and filed by hand. Clerks at this time were paid about $50 a month. The present interior is vastly different with computers, fax machines, internet communications, and touch-tone phones (replacing the rotary ones seen here).

POLICE DEPARTMENT ENTRANCE – CITY HALL, c.1955
50 Church St. • Built: 1937 • Architect: Robert Ian Macbeth (StC) • Builder: W.H. Yates Construction (Hamilton) • Designated 1978

Until the opening of the new City Hall, the St. Catharines Police force made its headquarters in a converted stable/carriage house that was part of the Clendennan/Benson house. Located next to the Market Square, it was likely built by the Benson family in the 1870s. When the new City Hall opened in 1937, the municipal offices (then in the former Clendennan/Benson house), the police offices, and the Municipal Court were relocated into the new building. In 1963, the police offices and court moved to the present Police Services Headquarters at 68 Church Street. The words over the door for the Police Department have since been removed.

PORT DALHOUSIE GAOL (JAIL), 1967
Lakeside Park Parking Lot (e. of Gary Rd.) • Built: c.1845 • Designated: 1979

The Port Dalhousie Jail, located next to Lakeside Park, is one of the oldest and smallest jails in Canada. Measuring only 4.6 m x 5.8 m (15'2½" x 19'2"), the jail consisted of two cells heated by a wood stove which prisoners would maintain themselves during cold weather. This tiny jail was used mainly as a temporary holding cell for rowdy sailors who had stopped at the lakeside port. For longer "stays" a larger jail was located in the village on Brock Street.

LINCOLN COUNTY JAIL, *c.*1975
116 Niagara St. • Built: 1866 (demolished 1976) • Architect: W.G. Storm (Toronto)

The Lincoln County Jail was in use from 1866 until the opening of the Niagara Regional Detention Centre in 1973. The jail was demolished three years later after much public debate. The jail's first occupant, Jack Bryant, was one of 164 other prisoners in its first year of operation. Despite the 76 cm (30″) thick walls, six escapes occurred during the jail's 107-year existence. Only one hanging took place at the Lincoln County Jail when Sidney Gordon Chambers was hung on December 16, 1947 for the murder of a 9-year-old St. Catharines girl.

CELL BLOCK – LINCOLN COUNTY JAIL, *c.*1975

A jail sentence in the late 19th century was focused less on rehabilitation, and more on incarceration and the punishment of inmates. Prisoners were assigned individual cells and their security was ensured through locks fitted deep within the limestone door frames, opened by a key on a small pole. Prisoners shared a common block with a sink, table, and toilet.

Central Fire Hall, c.1910
270 St. Paul St. • Built: 1867 (demolished 1953) • Architect: Thomas H. Wiley (StC) (1912 remodelling) • Builder: Samuel G. Dolson (StC)

Several large fires in the downtown prompted the decision to build a central fire hall at the corner of St. Paul and Carlisle (formerly Chesnut) Streets. Costing nearly $3,000, the four bays housed the steam pumpers, hose reels, horses, and the first motorized fire truck, purchased in 1917 (at which time their horses were retired from service). The hose-drying tower, not visible here, was damaged by a tornado in 1898 and was not rebuilt until 1912. Chief William Early, the first paid Fire Chief, lived upstairs with his family. The Fire Hall was closed in 1950 when the new one opened at the intersection of Geneva, Niagara, Queenston, and St. Paul Streets. Before its demolition in 1953, the vacant fire hall was used briefly to store the artifact collections of the Lincoln Historical Society. The most recent occupant of the new building at the fire hall site was the Berkshire Investment Group, closed as of 2005.

The Federal Building, *c.*1950
42 Queen St. • Built: 1883 (demolished *c.*1957-58) • Architect: Richard C. Windeyer (Toronto)

The first Federal Building in St. Catharines was built on the corner of King and Queen Streets, and was used as the Post Office and Customs House. It was designed in the Second Empire style. The Post Office was located on the ground floor and faced Queen Street (while the Customs House was upstairs with access off of King Street). When first built, the entire postal service consisted of a postmaster, an assistant postmaster, four clerks and one carrier. Delivery by postal carrier began in St. Catharines about 1910. After the First World War, the government assumed responsibility for post offices from privately operated postal operators, giving hiring preference to returning soldiers. The old Post Office closed in 1957 when the new one opened at 32 Church Street and was demolished about 1957-58 for construction of the Huron & Erie Canada Trust Company building.

ST. CATHARINES PUBLIC LIBRARY, 1914
55 Church St. • Built: 1905 (demolished 1977) • Architect: Sidney Rose Badgley (Cleveland, Ohio, formerly StC)

The first library in St. Catharines was housed in an Ontario Street building in 1877. It relocated in 1888 to Queen Street in the same building occupied by the *St. Catharines Standard*. The Library was destroyed by fire in 1895. Andrew Carnegie, a Scottish-American steel tycoon and philanthropist, donated money to build libraries. In total, he helped fund 2,509 libraries in 10 countries, of which 125 were in Canada. With funding from Carnegie, and the designs for the Greek Revival structure provided gratuitously by Sidney Rose Badgley, the Library officially opened on January 2, 1905. This was the municipality's first purpose-built library facility. It remained in use until the Centennial Public Library opened in 1977. It was then razed and the Provincial Courthouse erected in its place. Part of the columns and portico above the door are located on the grounds of the Centennial Library, and the owls in the foyer and main entrance. At the time of this photograph, the Library was decorated for the arrival in 1914 of Prince Arthur the Duke of Connaught (Canada's Governor-General), April 16, 1914.

MERRITTON PUBLIC LIBRARY, c.1949
344 Merritt St. • Built: 1924 • Architect: Arthur E. Nicholson (StC) • Designated: 1997

The first library in Merritton was formed in 1883 with quarters in the Town Hall. A grant from the Carnegie Corporation helped to fund construction of this building for the Merritton Public Library. It would be the second-last of 111 grants provided to Ontario communities between 1901 and 1917 (the grant for St. Catharines in 1901 was among the very first). It was built in the Neo-Tudor Arts and Crafts style, with decorative brickwork on the exterior facades. In 1968, the Merritton Library was closed and its services incorporated into the Pen Centre branch which had opened two years earlier. The Library building was then used as the Merritton Senior Citizens' Centre until 1995 when the Centre was relocated across the street to the renovated Town Hall. In 2005, the Norgen Biotek Corporation occupied the former Merritton Library building.

Montebello Park Bandstand, c.1904
Montebello Park (opp. 131-133 Ontario St.) • Built: 1904 • Builder: Edwin C. Nicholson (StC) • Designated 1978

Montebello Park was designed by Frederick Law Olmsted, "The Father of American Landscape Design," who also designed Central Park in New York City, and Mount Royal in Montreal. It was named Montebello, meaning "beautiful mountain", allegedly after an Italian village. An earlier bandstand, located near City Hall, was moved to the park in 1889. It was used for fifteen more years until this larger and more picturesque bandstand was built. The bandstand was modelled after one constructed for the 1901 Pan-American Exposition in Buffalo. Stately lions' heads, since disappeared, once adorned each of the supporting columns. The bandstand continues to host Sunday evening and special event concerts. In 2002, it was renamed The T. Roy Adams Bandshell in memory of the former mayor and musician.

St. Catharines Cemetery, pre-1897
480 Queenston St. • Built: 1856 (Cemetery) • Designated: 1994

Opened in 1856 as the St. Catharines Cemetery, it was renamed in 1897 in honour of Queen Victoria. Subsequent changes to the grounds include the addition of the iron gates in 1923, and the addition of the majestic Mills Memorial Carillon (tower), designed by Thomas R. Wiley, in 1949. Construction on the Cullinen Mausoleum – where the Burgoynes, Marquis, Newmans, and other prominent families are interred – was started in 1913 (with the first interment in 1916). Also interred on the grounds, and commemorated by a provincial plaque, is the Rev. Anthony Burns who was the fugitive slave of the 1854 Boston riots which resulted from his being taken back into captivity. His freedom was later purchased and he pastored at the Zion Baptist Church on Geneva Street in St. Catharines. The man in the foreground of this photo is thought to be Joseph Cameron, the Cemetery Superintendent.

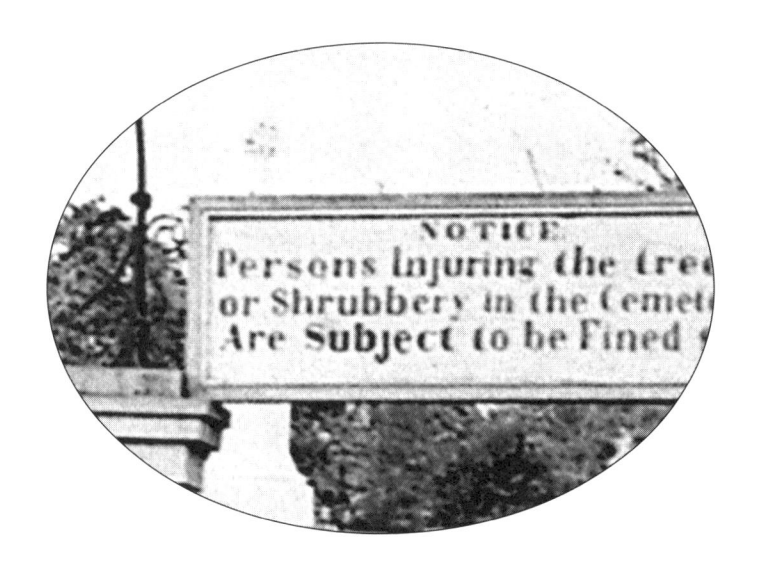

LAKE STREET ARMOURY, c.1910
81 Lake St. • Built: 1904-5 • Architect: The supervising local architect was S.G. Dolson • Builder: Sullivan & Langdon • Designated: 1996 (provincial)

The Armoury opened on May 23, 1906, with a two-day celebration. During the war years that followed soon after, it housed both infantry and artillery units and their associated equipment and accoutrements. Graham Thompson Lyall, a Victoria Cross recipient, enlisted here for service in the Great War. The Armoury continues to house The Lincoln and Welland Regiment, the 10th Field Battery, and the 68 Cadet Corps. Throughout the years, the Armoury has also hosted various events and exhibitions, including local horticultural fairs and auto shows.

#9 EFTS – HOSPITAL AND CANTEEN, 1942
Niagara Stone Rd. (now Niagara District Airport) • Built: 1942

Canada operated the nationwide British Commonwealth Air Training Plan (BCATP) to prepare pilots for service in the Second World War. Local lawyer and First World War pilot, Murton Seymour, was then enlisted to approach flying clubs across the country to help with the facilities, equipment, and personnel needed by the Air Force. The Elementary Flying Training School (#9 EFTS) graduated 1,848 pilots who went on to distinguished service in the RCAF and the RAF, including John Gillespie Magee, author of the poem *High Flight* – the official poem of the RCAF and RAF. The Hospital/Canteen was only one of 29 buildings added to the Flying Club's facilities as a result of improvements required for the wartime pilot-training program.

MILITARY CONVALESCENT HOME, c.1917
12 Yates St. • Built: 1860 • Architect: William Thomas (Toronto)

During the First World War, Miss Catharine Welland Merritt volunteered the Merritt dwelling for use as a convalescent home for wounded soldiers. At the time, 25 other convalescent homes were in operation across the country under the authority of the Canadian Military Hospitals Commission. Thousands of patients were treated, as well as being provided with vocational training to fit the men to suitable work. Other uses were later incorporated into the building until its purchase for CKTB radio, still in operation today (and featured elsewhere in this book).

NIAGARA PENINSULA SANATORIUM - NURSES' RESIDENCE, c.1950
541 Glenridge Ave. • Built: c.1930 • Architect: Whitten (Hamilton)

In 1905, Col. R.W. Leonard and his wife petitioned the Imperial Order Daughters of the Empire (IODE) to establish a hospital to care for patients with tuberculosis. The original St. Catharines Consumptive Sanatorium opened on October 19, 1909, on Collier Hill. Until 1911, when Dr. John Sheahan was appointed as a permanent part-time physician, doctors worked at the Sanatorium on a three-month rotation. In 1930 the Sanatorium was relocated to 541 Glenridge in order to provide beds for a greater number of patients. The Sanatorium was built at the top of the "San Hill" on Glenridge Avenue because the fresh air was considered healthier for patients. The Nurses' Residence was also built at that site, and two years later, Dr. C.G. Shaver added a medical library. In 1972, the building was designated a public hospital, and renamed the Shaver Hospital for Chest Diseases, now called the Hotel Dieu-Shaver Hospital.

ST. CATHARINES GENERAL AND MARINE HOSPITAL, c.1910
142 Queenston St. • Built: 1874

The first hospital in St. Catharines was founded by Dr. Theophilus Mack in 1865. It was built on Cherry Street and contained only four beds. A second hospital, on Hainer Street, opened two years later and was three times larger with twelve beds. In the spring of 1870, Dr. Mack purchased a plot of land on Queenston Street for the hospital's third expansion. The building in the photo is the former Winsor Chase home, built in the 1850's and sold by Chase in 1870. The building at the far left of the photo is believed to be the old nurses residence, built in 1874. The hospital provided 25 beds. While in 2005, over 200 beds were available for patient care to those from St. Catharines, Thorold, and Niagara-on-the-Lake. Its name was shortened in 1924 to the St. Catharines General Hospital and it is now a part of the enlarged Niagara Health System.

ST. CATHARINES GENERAL AND MARINE HOSPITAL, c.1911
While originally known as the St. Catharines General and Marine Hospital, in 1924 its name was shortened to the St. Catharines General Hospital. It is now part of the enlarged Niagara Health System. Its physical plant has also undergone many additions and alterations over the years. The construction project underway in this photo is believed to be for the "new hospital" (later known as the McSloy Wing). It was finished in 1911 by Newman Bros.

LEONARD HOME FOR NURSES, c.1925-30
154 Queenston St. • Built: 1924-25

The Leonard Home for Nurses was to be built west of the existing building of the St. Catharines General Hospital. It was instead built to the east, with enough room left between for a future wing to connect the two units. The home was named after Col. Reuben Wells Leonard, who joined the Board in 1916, and who helped finance its construction. Nurses lived on all four floors of the Home, and shared dining room, sitting room, and kitchen facilities. In 1972, the top two floors were demolished, and the remaining second floor was connected to the Moore Wing. In addition to housing the Chapel in 2005, offices for administration, laboratory, and pathology services are located there.

PROTESTANT ORPHANS' HOME, c.1934
172 Ontario St. • Built: 1877 (demolished 1951) • Architect: William B. Allan (StC)

The Protestant Orphans' Home was founded by The Ladies' Christian Association of St. Catharines to provide a refuge for the destitute, especially children and aged persons. Their first home, established in 1874 on Midland Street, soon proved inadequate. Thomas Rodman Merritt responded to their appeal for assistance by generously offering the land on Ontario Street, and $1,000 towards the erection of a suitable building, if they could raise a further $5,000. This goal was achieved and so the Italianate-style home was erected, opening in 1877. It appears very similar in design to St. Joseph's Convent on page 136. By 1900, the Home was caring solely for orphans. Orphans from foreign lands were also housed here, including those who escaped the Armenian Genocide in 1915. Condemned as unsafe in April 1949, the vacant building was purchased by the Religious Hospitallers. The building was demolished in 1951 and replaced by a parking lot for the Hotel Dieu Hospital.

WELLAND CANALS CENTRE / ST. CATHARINES MUSEUM, 2001

1932 Welland Canals Parkway (formerly Government Rd.) • Built: 1988-90; 1996-97 • Architect: Carlos Ventin (Simcoe) (1990); Baker & Elmes Architects (StC) (1997) • Builder: Merit Construction (StC) (1990); KCL Contracting & Engineering Ltd. (Mississauga) (1997)

When the Museum outgrew its historic home in the old Merritton Town Hall, it relocated to a custom-built, climate-controlled, state-of-the-art facility at Lock 3 on the Welland Ship Canal (a unique location which is only 23 metres (75') from an operating lock of the Seaway system). Partial operations at the newly-built Welland Canals Centre commenced in 1990, and it was officially opened on May 18, 1991 – *International Museums Day*. The Centre is attached to a Viewing Platform built by the St. Lawrence Seaway Authority in 1965, and is part of a complex that is one of the province's largest tourist attractions. The visitor's experience was enhanced with the addition of a wing in 1997 to house the Ontario Lacrosse Hall of Fame & Museum, the opening on the grounds of the Millennium Discovery Park in 2001, and the unveiling of the Welland Canals Interpretive Centre in June 2005. The gathering pictured above is for the 2001 Top Hat Ceremony, an event which annually recognizes the first upbound ship to transit the system at the start of a new shipping season.

Abbey: James S., 56; John P., 56; Rachel, Mrs., 56; William S., 56
Abbs, John, 43
Adams, T. Roy, Mayor, 148
Agriculture. *See also Horticulture;* DAIRIES; Avondale, 86; Avondale, 73; E.A. Bunting, 86; Ernest Cain, 86; Garden City, 86; Mason's, 86; McMahon's, 86; Sanitary, 86; Silverwood's, 86; Sunshine, 86; FLOUR & FEED; Archie Miller's Flour & Feed, 98; Byers Feed & Seed, 81; G.H. Mitchell Flour & Feed, 98; Harold Rayner Flour & Feed, 98; Moyer Bro's Flour & Feed, 81; Shur-Gain, 98; St. Catharines Feed Barn, 81; St. Catharines Flour & Feed, 98; St. Catharines Growers Co-op Feed Mill, 98; Titterington & Pay flour and feed, 53; Lincoln Canning Co., 97; Pay, John Albert (Bert), fruit grower, 53; Pay, William Henry, fruit grower, 53; Port Dalhousie Canning, 62, 116
Almon, H.L.A., Rev., 21
Anderson, J.E., 79
Andert, William, 88
Ansell, Charles A., 36
Apartments: Bayside Village, 135; Collier, 54; Merritt, The, 109
Architects: Allan, William B., 110, 137, 154; Badgley, Sidney Rose, 15, 109, 146; Beebe, M.C., 13; Chapman, Donald, 83; Dolson, Samuel G., 134; Ewart, David, 150; Fuller, T.W., 150; Graham, Charles J., 16; Haight, Samuel, 12; Hesson, Lionel A., 132; Hobson, Joseph, 25; Howard, John, 12; Latshaw, John, 75, 138; Macbeth & Williams, 14; Macbeth, Robert Ian, 12, 141, 142; Macdonald & Zuberec, 38, 42; Maw, Samuel H., 62; Mirynech, Michael, 9; Morgan, Earl C., 100; Nicholson & Macbeth, 13, 70, 79, 131; Nicholson, Arthur E., 12, 147; Olmsted, Frederick Law, 148; Panici, Venerino P.P., 9; Richardson, R.R., 13; Robinson, Gerald, Dr., 13; Ruh, Philip, Rev., 24; S.B. Coon & Son, 119; Salter & Fleming, 42; Salter, Wilson A., 131, 132; Sauder, Grant, 24; Sproat & Rolph, 18; Stewart & Whitton, 128; Stone, H.C., 65; Storm, W.G., 143; Thomas, William, 40, 151; Travers, Lewis, 52; Tully, Kivas, 61, 138; Ventin, Carlos, 155; Walton, F.T., 9; Whitten, 151; Wiley, Thomas H., 45, 73, 78, 89, 126, 129, 144; Wiley, Thomas R., 38, 102, 149; Wilson, William M., 133; Windeyer, Richard C., 145; Zeidler, Eberhard H., 83
Architecture: Art Deco, 88, 141; Arts & Crafts Movement, 16; Byzantine Revival, 24; Doric, 119; English, 44; Georgian, 58; Georgian, early, 121; Gothic, 9; Gothic Revival, 12, 16; Gothic, Old English, 15; Gothic, Perpendicular, 18; Greek Revival, 146; Italianate, 15, 38, 40, 135, 154; Las Vegas, 67; Medieval, 16; Neo-Classic, 40; Neo-Romanesque, 70; Neo-Tudor, 70, 79; Neo-Tudor Arts & Crafts, 147; Renaissance Revival, 42, 61; Richardson Romanesque, 13; Romanesque, 14; Second Empire, 117; Tudor, 14, 121; Victorian, 123
Art & Artists. *See also Photographers;* Suhacev, Igor, 24; Tinkler, Chris, 16
Arthur, Prince, Duke of Connaught, 129, 146
Associations & Societies: American Institute of Architects, 18; Friends of Malcolmson Park, The, 34; Friends of Morningstar Mill, 101; Heritage St. Catharines, 58; Hunt Club, 38; Imperial Order Daughters of the Empire (IODE), 151; Independent Order of Oddfellows (IOOF), 50, 53, 79, 108; Islamic Society of St. Catharines, 24; Ladies' Christian Association of St. Catharines, 154; Lincoln Agricultural Society, 53; Lincoln Historical Society, 144; Masonic Memorial Temple, 125; Merritton Lions Club, 137; Ontario Undertakers' Association, 50; Port Dalhousie Lions Club, 116; Religious Hospitallers of St. Joseph, 39; St. Catharines & District Arts Council, 42; St. Catharines Rotary Club, 36, 74; Temple Lodge of Masons, 43; Welland Canals Preservation Association, 91; Welland Canals Society, 91, YMCA, YM-YWCA, 70
Automobiles, 28, *See also Bus Service, Highways;* Alex's (garage), 98; Automotive dealership and tire repair, 24; Canada Pole & Shaft, 102; Canada Wheel Works, 102; Canadian Oil Companies, 60; Conroy Mfg., 88; Epp's Service Centre, 98; General Motors, 89; Golchuk, William (garage), 98; Golchuk's, 98; Haney Auto Service, 29; Hayes-Dana, 102; Kelsey-Hayes, 88; McKinnon Industries, 91; Reo Motor Car Co., 74; St. Catharines Tire Company, 59; Sun Collision, 110; Two-way traffic, St. Paul St., 69; U.S.-Canada Automotive Trade Pact, 102
Aviation. *See also Military, Wars;* Airport Inn, 29; British Commonwealth Air Training Plan (BCATP), 150; Elementary Flying Training School (EFTS), 150; Magee, John Gillespie, *High Flight*, 150; Niagara District Airport, 29; Seymour, Murton, 150

Babayan, Levan, 19
Banks & Banking: Alliance Paper Company Credit Union, 106; Bank of Nova Scotia, 43, 65; Canada Trust, 83; CIBC, 60; Huron & Erie Canada Trust Company, 145; Lincoln Trust House, 83; Niagara District Bank, 60; RBC Financial Services, 74; Security Loan & Savings Co., 71; Sovereign Bank of Canada, 65
Barber, John V., 107
Barley, Ald., 54
Baston, John E., 54
Bate, Thomas B., 87
Bennett, R.B., PM, 75
Benson, James Rae, Sen., 42, 60, 97, 140; Mary, 42
Birchall, Leonard, 129
Black, John L., 51; Robert M., 73
Blacks: Anti-slavery legislation, 1793, 10; Burns, Anthony, Rev., 149
Blacksmiths: Cratt, William F., 99; Matthews, Tom, 82; Stocking, Jerry, 99; Wilson, J., 99
Bonnet, Hannah, 51
Borecky, Isidore, Bishop, 24
Brantford: F.C. Burroughes Furniture Store, 69
Brewers: Carling-O'Keefe, 87; Silver Spire, 41; Taylor & Bate, 41, 87
Bridges: Burgoyne, 79
Bryant, Jack, 143
Buffalo: Crawford family, 57; Pan-American Exposition, 1901, 148
Builders: Barron, William, 138; Burgoyne, Henry, 15; Clyde, John, 75, 117; Dolson, Samuel G., 12, 15, 22, 138, 144; Dougan, James, Sr., 122; Drysdale & Kirby, 133; Garbitt, Victor, 24; Garson & Purcer, 107; George Wilson & Co. Planing Mill & Box Factory (*see also* Wilson, George), 113; Gilleland, James, 12; Haight, Samuel, 12, 140; Holmes, Daniel W., 132; J.R. Stork & Son, 133; KCL Contracting & Engineering, 155; Lord & Burnham, 34; McDonald, James, 137; Merit Construction, 155; Newman Bros., 21, 65, 89, 125, 126, 129, 131, 134, 152; Nicholson, Edwin C., 148; Pay, William, 140; Roger Miller & Son, 27; Rymer Bros., 107, 132; Sullivan, Timothy, 13; Switzer, Edwin, 110; T.R. Hinan Contractors, 9; Thompson, Richard, 55; W.H. Yates Construction, 119, 141, 142; Walker, John, 137; Walton, F.T., 9; Waud, Godfrey, 12, 46; Wilson, George (*see also* George Wilson & Co. Planing Mill & Box Factory), 16
Buildings, materials: Bedford stone, 18; British Columbia cedar, 18; Florida Cypress, 75; Georgetown stone, 18; gumwood, 63; Kingston stone, 9; marble, 44; red Queenston limestone, 13, 16, 17, 106, 110; terrazzo, 141; Tyndall limestone, 28
Burgoyne: Bill, 41, 54; Henry, 15; Henry B., 41; Interment, 149; William B., 72
Burns, Anthony, Rev., 149; R.F., Rev., 14
Burnstein, Louis, 87; Sam, 54
Burtch, George, 91
Bus service, 28
Businesses. *See also Agriculture, Architects, Art & Artists, Automobiles, Banks & Banking, Blacksmiths, Brewers, Communications, Dentists, Department Stores, Developers, Health Spas, Horticulture, Hotels, Industries, Mills, Newspapers. Photographers, Physicians & Doctors, Restaurants & Diners;* Algoma Central, 136; Alice's Antiques, 84; BUTCHERS; Carry Market, 80; Hocking's Meat Market, 80; Payne's Meat Market, 80; Canada Life Assurance, 73; CLOTHING; Denton's Tailor Shop, 111; Jack Nash Men's Wear, 68; Sal's Place, 67; Susan Miles Ltd., 64; Cremation Centre Inc., 81; Downtown Dental Centre, 69; Durward, Jones, Barkwell, 74; Enbridge Gas, 123; Forget-Me-Knot Antiques, 84; FURNITURE & APPLIANCES; F.C. Burroughes Furniture Store, 69; Finnegan's Upholstery, 109; Frigidaire, 74; Sleep Factory, The, 76; Star Appliances, 109; GROCERS; Carroll's Ltd., 80; John Wood's, 111; Loblaw's, 123; Phelan's, 73; Roddy & Walker, 96; Stanton's, 114; Welsh & Company Wholesale, 76; Williams, 96; H.E. Rose & Co., 74; Hamdani Enterprises, 88; Hansa Imports, 84; Holly's Candy Store, 64; Hughson Business, 83; ICN, 49; Kennash Corporation, 67; Milk Maid Shoppe, 108; MUSIC; Dominion Music Store, 71; Dominion Organ & Piano, 71; Mason & Risch Pianos, 115; Niagara Recycling, 102; Norgen Biotek Corporation, 147; Park Fruit Store, 73; Picasso's Hair Salon, 117; Sally McGarr Realty, 60; St. Catharines & Welland Canal

Gas Light, 97; Station to Station, 78; Studio 76, 44; Synergy Benefits Consulting Inc., 81; Titterington Co. Ltd. Wholesale Produce, 98; Wardell & Son Moving Contractors, 23; Williams Jewellers, 78; Wise Lumber Company, 59

Cairn, James, 66
Cameron, Joseph, 149
Campbellville: Mohawk Raceway, 100
Carmichael, Harry J., 88
Carnegie Corporation, 147; Carnegie, Andrew, 146
Cavell, Edith, 130
Cemeteries: Anglican (PtD), 22; Cullinen Mausoleum, 149; St. Catharines Cemetery, 149; St. George's Church (formerly the Church at St. Catharines), 12; Victoria Lawn, 149
Chambers, Sidney Gordon, 143
Chapman, William J., Dr., & Gladys, 45
Chisholm, William A., 97
Churches. *See also Ministers, Mosques, Religion*; African Methodist Episcopal (AME), 10; Armenian Mission of St. Catharines, 19; British Methodist Episcopal (BME), 10; Christ Anglican, 13; Christ Church (McNab), 23; Church at St. Catharines, the, 12; Church of Scotland, 22; Elm Street Methodist (United), 21; First Baptist, 14; First Presbyterian (United), 20, 43; Grace Methodist, 15; Grantham Baptist, 14; Grantham United, 20; Knox Presbyterian, 14; Mary, Star of the Sea R. C. (formerly Our Lady of the Lake R.C.), 9; Our Lady of the Lake R.C., 9; Pine Street Wesleyan, 21; Ridley Memorial Chapel, 18; Southridge Community, 132; St. Andrew's Methodist (United), 22; St. Barnabas Anglican, 16; St. Barnabas Mission Chapel, 16; St. Catherine of Alexandria R.C., 11, 38, 82, 136; St. George's Anglican (formerly the Church at St. Catharines), 12; St. Gregory The Illuminator Armenian Apostolic, 19; St. James Anglican, 21; St. John's Anglican, 22; St. John's Roman Catholic, 11; St. Mary of the Assumption, 17; St. Paul Street Methodist (United) (formerly Wesleyan Methodist Church), 15; St. Thomas' Anglican, 13, 18; Sts. Cyril & Methodius Ukrainian Catholic, 24, 131; United Church of Canada, 15, 21, 22; Welland Avenue Methodist (United), 15; Wesleyan Methodist Church, 15; Zion Baptist, 149
Churchill, Winston, Sir, 62, 132
Civil Defense, 137; Emergency Measures Organization, 123
Clapp, Roy E., 68
Clark, John, Lt.-Col., 58
Clendennan, James, 140
Coleman, A.E., 87
Colleges & Universities. *See also Schools*; Brock University, 42, 117; Magdalen College, 15; Ontario College of Pharmacy, 43; University of Toronto, 47, 120; Wycliffe College, 120
Collier Hill, 151
Collier's Hall, 16
Collinson, Samuel, 91
Communications. *See Radio & Radio Broadcasting, Telegraph*
Concrete Poles: world's tallest, 32
Conlon: John, 105; John J., 49; John J. & Margaret, 48; Thomas & Anne, 49
Conner, John, 109
Conroy, John, 88
Cook, Moses, 37
Cooke, William, 32
Coombs, A.E. 'Scout', 118
Coyle, Leo, 78
Cratt, William E., 99
Crawford: George B. & Lucy, 57; George Ralston, 57; James & Margaret, 57
Crimes & Criminals. *See also Jails, Law, Police*; murder of Sam Stinson, 66

Davis, Bette, 62; Davis, Jefferson, Pres., 75
Day Care Centre. *See also Schools*; Kids Place Child Care Centre, 131
Dentists. *See also Physicians & Doctors*; Harley, Blake, Dr., 111; Hrabowsky, Ivan, Dr., 69
Department Stores: James D. Tait dry goods, 61; McLaren's dry goods store, 62; Phillips Department Store, 69; S.S. Kresge Company Limited, 61; T. Eaton Co., 62; Twin Fair Department Store, 69; Woolworths Corporation, 63

Derderian, Hovnan, Archbishop, 19
Developers: Baston, John E., 54; Merritton Development, 106; Merritton Mills Redevelopment Corp., 105
Dingle family, 29
Diseases: cholera (St. George's), 12
Dittrick: Duncan & Martha, 51; Jacob & Margaret, 51; Robert & Hannah, 51
Downtown: traffic congestion, 27
Duff, John, 107
Dunn, Bob, 107; R.L., 93
Dwyer, Eugene F., 114

Early, William, Chief, 144
Eden, Anthony, Sir, 62
Education. *See Day Care Centre, Colleges & Universities, School Boards, Schools*
Eisenhower, Dwight D., 62
Electricity: DeCew Generating Station, 100; Dominion Electric, 47; Ferranti Electric, 90; Hydro Commission, 137; Lincoln Electric Light & Power, 32; Lincoln Transformer Station, 32; McSloy residences (Hugh & James), 38; Ontario Hydro, 32, 101; Ontario Power Generation, 100; Packard Electric, 47, 90; St. Catharines Public Utilities Commission (PUC), 32
Elevators, 38
Elizabeth II, Queen, 141
Elizabeth, Queen Mother, 62
Elliott, J.S., 128
Entertainment. *See also Events, Music & Musicians*; Montebello Park Bandstand, 148
Ethnic Groups. *See also Blacks*; Armenians, 19, 154; Folk Arts Council Multicultural Centre, 118; German, 25; Irish, 11; Muslim, 24; Turkey, 19; Ukrainian; Church, 24; School, 131
Events. *See also Entertainment, Music & Musicians*; Coronation of Queen Elizabeth II, 1953, 141; Feast Day of St. John the Baptist, 22; International Museums Day, May 18, 155; Kiwanis Horse Show, 100; Opening of St. Lawrence Seaway, 1959, 141; Pan-American Exposition, 1901, 148; Proclamation of Christianity in Armenia, 1700th Anniversary, 19

Finlay, Edward, 87; William, 87
Fires & Firefighting: Central Fire Hall, 59, 144; Early, William, Chief, 144; GWR Station, 25; Grand Opera House, 77; Hippodrome, 64; IOOF Lodge, 79; Lakeside Park Dance Pavilion, 116; Maple Leaf Rubber, 112; May-Clark Home, 58; Merritton Fire Hall, Town Hall, 137; Morningstar Mill, 101; Oak Hill, 40; Phelps Mill, 104; Queen Street Baptist Church, 14; Queen Street Library, 146; Ridley College Rink, 121; Russell House, 66; Springbank Hotel, 120; St. Catherine of Alexandria Church, 11; St. George's Church, 12; St. Gregory The Illuminator Armenian Apostolic Church, 19; St. James Anglican Church, 21; St. Joseph's Convent, 136; St. Paul Street Methodist Church, 15; Whitman & Barnes Knife Works, 91
Fonthill: NS&T, 27
Franklin, John, Ald., 54
Fretz, Chris, 116

Gamble, Robert Francis, 114
Gibb, John, 44
Gilleland, William & Annie, 37
Glackmeyer, Edward, 97
Golchuk, Alex, 98; William, 98
Government: COUNTY; Children's Shelter, 37; Lincoln County Courthouse, 138; Lincoln County Industrial Home, 53; FEDERAL, 32, *See also Postal Services, Military, St. Lawrence Seaway, Welland Canals*; Department of Public Works, 31; Department of Railways & Canals, 35; Federal Building, Post Office & Customs House, 145; Post Office, 70, 71; MUNICIPAL; Amalgamation, 46, 52, 137; Justice of the Peace, 71; Merritton; Public Utilities Commission (PUC), 107; Town Hall, 137, 147, 155; Waterworks, 107; Waterworks Commission, 137; St. Catharines; Children's Shelter, 37; City Clerk, 53; City Clerk's Office, 141; City Council, 43; City Hall, 140, 141, 142, 148; Emergency Measures Organization (EMO), 123; Public Utilities Commission (PUC), 32; Town Hall, 139, 140; Waterworks: Merritton, 107, 137; REGIONAL; Niagara Land Division, 123; Public Works, 123; Region Niagara Waterworks, 107

157

Gowan, Nassau W., 71
Grammar, Peter, 63
Grant, Alexander Joseph, 35
Grantham Township: Gilleland, 37; Hack Farm, 33; Pay, J. Albert, 53; Pay, William H., 53; survey patterns, 84
Greenhouses. *See Horticulture*
Greenwood, W.T., Dr., 44; William, 49, 73
Gregory, Johnson I., 114

Hack, Ernest H., 33
Hallett, Robert E., 108
Hamdani, Hussein A., 24; Mohammed H., 24
Hamilton: Great Western Railway, 26; Hughson Business, 83
Hamilton, Ralph B., 117
Haney, Jack, 29
Hardy, Ann, 73
Harley, Blake, Dr., 111
Harper, Martha, 51
Hart, Wilfred Laurier, 114
Hawken: Edwin & Mary Ann, 47; Gertrude, 47; Isabella, 47; James, 47; Robert E., 47
Hawley, Estelle Cuffe, 117
Health Spas: Springbank Hotel, 85, 120, 121; Stephenson House, 75, 85; Welland House, 41, 75, 85
Henley Island, 32
Heritage Designations: NATIONAL HISTORIC SITES; BME Church, 10; Lake St. Armoury, 140; PROVINCIAL; BME Church, 10; City Hall, 140, 141, 142; Lake Street Armoury, 150; Locktenders' Shanty, 30; Merritton Library, 147; Merritton Town Hall, 137, 155; Montebello Park Bandstand, 148; Moringstar Mill, 101; Murphy's, 111; Old Courthouse, 138; Port Dalhousie Jail, 142; Russell House (de-designated), 66; St. Paul Street Methodist Church, 15; Sts. Cyril & Methodius Church, 24, 131; Victoria Lawn Cemetery, 149; Waud-Norris House, 46; Yates Street Heritage District, 46; HERITAGE CONSERVATION DISTRICTS-Port Dalhousie, June 17, 2002 & March 3, 2003; Queen Street, April 29, 1991; Yates Street, September 11, 1995
Highways. *See also Automobiles, Bus Service;* Highway 406, 31, 51, 87, 92; Highway 8, 29; QEW, 29
Hill, William A., 68
Hoffman, Ralph J., 64
Holder, John, 93
Holmes, M., Miss, 128
Homer: Airport, 29; J. Wilson Blacksmith Shop, 99
Horticulture. *See also Agriculture, Parks;* Dunn, R.L., 93; Rosebank Nursery (Holder, John), 93; W.W. Walker & Sons, Florist, 62; Welland Canals; Forestry Dept., 35; Greenhouse, Lock 1, 34
Hospitals: Cherry Street, 152; De Veaux Hall, 39; Delta Medical Arts, 96; Hainer Street, 152; Hospital / Canteen #9 EFTS, 150; Hotel Dieu, 39, 154; Hotel Dieu-Shaver Hospital, 151; Leonard Home for Nurses, 153; McSloy Wing, Gen. Hosp., 152; Military Convalescent Home, 151; Niagara Health System, 152; Niagara Peninsula Sanatorium, 151; Springbank Sanatorium, 120; St. Catharines Consumptive Sanatorium, 151; St. Catharines General, 71, 152, 153
Hotels. *See also Restaurants & Diners;* Grand Central, 67; Leonard, 70; Lincoln, 67; Montebello Inn, 67; Murray House, 83; New Murray, 83; Pickwick House, 83; Railway Hotel (Merritton), 25; Russell House, 66; Springbank, 85, 120; Stephenson House, 75, 85; Thompson, 111; Welland House, 41, 75, 85; Wood House (PtD), 111, 114
Howe, Elias, 94
Hrabowsky, Ivan, Dr., 69
Hunter, doug, PUC, 54
Hutton, Richard, 30

Industries. *See also Businesses, Mills;* Canada Hair Cloth, 38; Canada Knife Works, 91; City Gas Works, 97; Conroy Mfg., 88; Dominion Electric, 47; Dominion Hair Cloth, 73; Dominion Tungsten Lamp Factory, 47; Empire Carpet Works, 95; Empire Rug Mills, 95; Ferranti Electric, 90; Ferranti-Packard, 90; Foster Wheeler, 95; General Motors, 89; Jenckes Engineering & Machine Works of Canada, 95; Kelsey-Hayes, 88; Lightning Fastener, 94; Lincoln Foundry, 87; Lowe & Boylan's Carriage Factory, 82; McKinnon Dash & Hardware, 89; McKinnon Industries, 91; MERRITTON; Canada Pole & Shaft, 102; Canada Wheel Works, 102; Hayes-Dana, 102; Independent Rubber, 106; Pioneer Pole & Shaft, 102; Shawinigan Chemical, 103; Willson Carbide Works, 103; NuCon Holdings, 94; Packard Electric, 47, 90; Paxton & Bray Brick Yard, 54; PORT DALHOUSIE; Consolidated Rubber, 106, 113; Lincoln Fabrics, 113; Maple Leaf Rubber, 112; Reo Motor Car Co., 74; Talon, 94; Textron, 94; Trenergy, 95; Whitman & Barnes, 91, 110
Inventions: Gowan Safety Device, 71; Refrigerators, 115; Zipper, 94

Jacobson, Oscar F., 132
Jails. *See also Crimes & Criminals, Law, Police;* Niagara Regional Detention Centre, 143; Port Dalhousie, 142; Town Hall (Merritton), 147; Town Hall (StC), 143
Jameson, William, 134
Jones, Robert Trent, 92
Judson, Whitcomb L., 94

Kane, M.J., 73
Karekin II, 19
Karn, Charles, 84; Harry, 84
Kazmir, John, 44
Keating, Michael Y., 71
Kelly, A., 114
Kowal, Jerry, 66

Larkin, Patrick, 105
Latcham, Bill, 111
Law. *See also Crimes & Criminals, Jails, Police;* Lincoln County Courthouse, 138; Municipal Court, 142; Provincial Courthouse, 146; Victoria Hall, 138; Welland Courthouse, 138
Lawrie, John, 112; Robert, 112
Leavenworth, Hiram, 49
Lennox, B.M., Dr., 45
Leonard, R.W., Col., 70, 151, 153
Lewkowitz, I., Dr., 44
Libraries: MERRITTON; Carnegie, 137, 147; Public, 147; ST. CATHARINES; Carnegie, 45, 146; Ontario Street, 146; Public, 82; Queen Street, 146
Lyall, Graham Thompson, V.C., 150

MacDonald, Ramsay, PM, 75
Mack, Caroline, 44; Theophilus, Dr., 85, 120, 152
Macleod, V.D., 43
Magee, John Gillespie, 150
Main, Hugh J., 108
Malls & Plazas: Corbloc, 83; Geneva Square, 28; Grantham Plaza, 68; Midtown Plaza, 28, 69; Pen Centre, 62, 147; Ridley Heights Plaza, 53
Market: Market Square, 139, 142; Public Weigh Scales, 139
Martindale Pond: Third Canal, 30
Martindale, John H., 114
May, William, 58; William. Jr., 58
McArthur, George A., 135
McAvoy, Henry, Sr., 30
McCleary, 110
McCulley, Ernest I., 124, 132
McDonald, Angus, 100
McGuire, Mike, 60
McIlwain,Thomas, 78
McIntyre, John Brewer, 50; Thomas & Helen, 50
McKinnon, Lachlan Ebenezer, 89
McLean, 110
McSloy, Hugh & Anna, 38; James & Bessie, 38
Merritt: Catharine Welland, Miss, 151; Emily Alexandrina, 40; Jedediah P., 76; Thomas Rodman, 42, 60, 110, 154; William Hamilton, Dr., 42; William Hamilton, Jr., 42, 97; William Hamilton, the Hon., 10, 40, 42, 60, 61, 90
Merritton, 147; Cenotaph, 137; Central Public School, 134; Elm Street Church, 21; Fire Hall, 137; G.W.R. Station, 25; Glory Hill, 21; Hayes-Dana Ltd., 102; Main's Drug Store, 108; Police, 137; Senior Citizens' Centre, 147; St. James Anglican Church, 21; Thompson House, 55; Tornado, 1898, 55, 105, 133; Town Hall, 137; Willson Carbide Works, 103
Military. *See also Aviation, Wars;* 10th Field Battery, 150; 68 Cadet Corps, 150; Birchall, Leonard, 'Saviors of Ceylon', 129; Butler's Rangers, 58; Canadian Military Hospitals Commission, 151; Cannons, City Hall, 140; Cavell, Edith, WW I nurse, 130; Convalescent Home, 151; Lake Street Armoury, 140, 150; Lincoln & Welland Regiment, The, 150; Lyall, Graham

158

Thompson, V.C., 150; Magee, John Gillespie, 150; Seymour, Murton, 150; Soldiers, 26; Watson, Alexander, Pvt., 140
Miller, George, 52
Milligan, Cecil W., Capt., 96
Mills: COTTON; Beaver Cotton, 106; Lybster, 105; Merritton Cotton, 106; FLOUR & GRIST; Moringstar Mill, 101; Neelon Mill, 90; Norris & Neelon, 112; Norris Roller Mills, 87; R.&J. Lawrie, 112; PAPER; Alliance Paper Mills, 105; Domtar, 105, 106; International Paper Co., 110; Kimberly-Clark, 110; Kinleith Paper, 87; Lincoln Paper Mills, 105; Lybster, 105; Riordon Paper Mill, 91; SAW; McCleary & McLean, 110; Phelps Mill, 104
Mills, David Bloss, 70; James, 70
Ministers. *See also Churches, Religion;* Almon, H.L.A., Rev., 21; Borecky, Isidore, Bishop, 24; Buell, A.K., Rev., 20; Burns, Anthony, Rev., 149; Burns, R.F., Rev., 14; Derderian, Hovnan, Archbishop, 19; Fulton, Thomas J., Most Rev., 11; Harris, W.R., Very Rev., 11; Karekin II, 19; McIntosh, Angus, 22; Phillips, Thomas D., Rev., 122; Rose, Hugh, Rev., 46; Ruh, Philip, Rev., 24; Wilson, George, Dr., 14
Mitchell, F.F., 89
Mittleberger, Henry, 14
Mittlefehldt, Frank, 130
Monuments & Memorials: Cenotaph, Merritton, 137; Memorial Public School, 130; Mills Memorial Carillon, 149; Ridley Memorial Chapel, 18; Watson Monument, 140
Moore, Daniel, 105
Moote, Dorothy, Miss, 131
Morningstar, Wallace, 101; Wilson, 101
Morrison, Ashton, 127
Mosques. *See also Churches;* MASJID an-NOOR Mosque, 24
Movies & Plays. *See also Theatres, Poems; A Christmas Story,* 127; *A Nugget of Gold,* 64; *The Price of Silence,* 78
Moyer, Lewis, 81
Muller, F.A., 45
Murphy, Edward, 111; Wilfred, 111
Murray, James, Capt., 83
Museums: Morningstar Mill, 101; Ontario Lacrosse Hall of Fame, 155; Rodman Hall, 37, 42, 61; St. Catharines, 66, 137, 138, 155; Welland Canals Interpretive Centre, 155
Music & Musicians. *See also Entertainment;* Adams, T. Roy, Bandshell, 148; Montebello Park Bandstand, 148; Niagara Conservatory of Music, 125

Nash, Dave, 68; Harold, 68; Maurice, 68
Neelon, Sylvester, 90, 105
New York City: Crawford family, 57
Newspapers: Buffalo *Courier,* 110; CanWest Global, 72; *Evening Star,* 72; *Farmers' Journal & Welland Canal Intelligencer,* 49; Hamilton *Spectator,* 110; *Montreal Witness,* 110; Osprey Media Group, 72; Quebec *Chronicle,* 110; Southam, 72; *St. Catharines Journal,* 72; St. Catharines Standard, 54, 65, 72, 146; *The Globe,* 110; *The Mail,* 110; *The Mail & Empire,* 110; *Weekly Telegraph and Sun,* 110
Niagara Falls: F.C. Burroughes Furniture Store, 69; Great Western Railway, 26; Mason & Risch Pianos, 115; NS&T, 27
Niagara-on-the-Lake: BME Church, 10; NS&T, 27
Nice, Ward F., 107
Norris, James, Capt., 14, 46

O'Keefe, John, 66
O'Loughlin, Kathleen, 44; Mary, 44
O'Mara, Hubert, 97
Office Buildings: Algoma Central, 136; Corbloc, 83; Lincoln Trust House, 83; Misener, 136; Prendergast Block, 61; Taro, 45
Orphans. *See Social Services*
Ottawa: Phillips School, 122

Paget, 29; Thomas, 59; Tom, Jr., 59
Parks: Grimsby, 104; Lakeside, 116; Malcolmson, 34; Millennium Discovery, 155; Montebello, 42, 43, 148; Welland Canal Greenhouse, 34
Parnall, William, 54
Pattison, Fred, 29
Pawling, Nathan, 114
Paxton, John, 30
Pay: John Albert (Bert), 53; Kate Boyle, 53; Sarah, 53; William Henry, 53

Peak, Robert, 37
Penner, Ernest, 73
Petrie, Harry & Emma, 96
Phelan, 73
Phelps, Noah, 104; Oliver, 10, 20, 90; Orson, 14, 104
Phelpston, 104
Phillips, Thomas D., Rev., 122
Photographers. *See also Art & Artists.* Caplan, Frank, 30, 32, 36, 62, 76, 80, 86, 105, 136, 143; Card, A.S., 95; Dept. of Railways & Canals, 34; Goodman, Harry C., 43, 146; Hamdani, Hussein, 24; International Stationery, 39; James & Son, 18; Leslie, F.H., 21, 128, 134; Miller, Wilfred A.L., 31, 32, 41, 101, 142; Poole, Edwin C., 38, 65, 71, 77, 104; Rumsey & Co., 12, 14, 15, 27; Schwenger, Kathryn, 100; See, Joseph T., 20; Shaw, Dave, 155; Sinclair, Don *(St. Catharines Standard),* 54, 88, 95; Snider, Lloyd, 152; Valentine & Sons Publishing, 13, 14, 16, 121, 138; Valentine-Black Co. Ltd., 75; Villiers, Will, 60; Willis, Winnifred M., 96; Wilson, John, 99
Physicians & Doctors. *See also Dentists;* Chapman, William J., Dr., 45; Greenwood, W.T., Dr., 44; Lennox. B.M, Dr., 45; Lewkowitz, I., Dr., 44; Mack, Theophilus, Dr., 85, 120, 152; Shaver, C.G., Dr., 151; Sheahan, John, Dr., 151
Pickard, Margaret, 51
Pierce, George W., 117
Poems. *See Also Movies & Plays; High Flight,* 150
Police, 137, *See also Crimes & Criminals, Jails, Law;* Lincoln County Courthouse, 138; Merritton Town Hall, 137; Police Headquarters, 139, 142; Police Station, 38; St. Catharines Police Force, 142
Port Colborne: NS&T, 27
Port Dalhousie, 106; Abbey, William S., 56; Crawford residence, 57; Ice House, 115; Locktenders' Shanty, 30; Martindale Pond, 115; Mary, Star of the Sea R.C. Church, 9; Merry-go-Round, 116; Muir Bros. Dry Dock, 36; NS&T, 116; Port Dalhousie City Gas Works, 97; Port Dalhousie Jail, 142; Port Dalhousie Public School, 135; post office, 114; Reeve, first, 112; Scouts, 116; Shell House, 32; St. Andrew's Presbyterian Church, 22; St. John's Anglican Church, 21, 22
Port Hope, 88
Port Weller: Fourth Welland Canal Opening, 30
Postal Services, 9; Federal Building, Customs House, 49, 145; Merritton, 137; Port Dalhousie, 114; Post Office, 70, 71
Prior, James, 73

Queen Street Baptist Church, 14
Quinn, John, 66

Radio & Radio Broadcasting. *See also Telegraph;* 105.7 EZ Rock, 41; 97.7 HTZ-FM, 41; CKTB, 40, 41, 87, 151; Radio antenna, first vertical, 41; Silver Spire Broadcasting Station Ltd., 41
Railways. *See also Street Railways;* Canadian National, 26, 28; Grand Trunk, 25, 26; Great Western, 25, 26
Ranney, John L., 97
Read, Richard, 30
Religion. *See also Churches, Ministers, Mosques;* Crucifixion, 9; Religious Hospitallers, 154; Sisters of St. Joseph, 154; Virgin Mary, 9
Residences: Abbey, William, 56; Chapman, William J., Dr., 45; Clark, John, Lt. Col., 58; Clendennan/Benson, 141; Collier Apartments, 54; Conlon, John J., 48; Conlon, Thomas, 49; Cook, Moses, 37; Crawford, 57; Dittrick, Jacob, 51; Gilleland, William & Annie, 37; Greenwood, W.T., Dr., 44; Greenwood, William, 49; Hawken, 40; May, William, 58; McIntyre, Thomas, 50; McSloy, Hugh, 38; McSloy, James, 38; Merritt, 40; Miller, 52; Norris, James, Capt., 46; O'Loughlin, 44; Oak Hill, 40; Pay, Albert J., 53; Rodman Hall, 42; Shickluna, Louis, 41; Suncroft, 38; Thompson, Richard, 55; Walker, James N., 43; Walnut Dale Farm, 58; Waud, Godfrey, 46; Westchester Place, 37; Woodruff, Samuel D., 39; Woodruff, Welland, 39
Restaurants & Diners: Airport Inn, 29; Astoria, 80; Coppola's Ristorante, 97; Crystal Coffee Shop, 96; Diana Sweets, 63; Fortis' Family, 96; Hallett's Coach House, 108; Hospital / Canteen, 150; Kaz's Pub, 63; Mai Vi, 61; Mansion House, 109; Merritton Tavern, 109; Murphy's, 111; Oasis Middle East Cuisine, 64; Ricci's Tavern, 109; Sahla Thai, 67; Shtoynkas Sandwiches, 63; Star, 80; Stella's, 80; The Keg, 106; Union Tavern, 108

Richardson: Belle; Claude; Edith; Frank; William A., 109
Richmond, Robert, 73
Ridley, Nicholas, Bishop, 120
Riordon, Charles, 110; John, 110, 137
Robertson, Dick, Mayor, 54
Rose, Howard E., 74; Hugh, Rev., 46
Royalty: Duke of Connaught, Prince Arthur, Governor General, 129, 146; Elizabeth, Queen Mother, 62; Queen Elizabeth II, 141; Queen Victoria, 149

Sandell, E.T., 40
Sargeant, Emery, 66
School Boards: Merritton School Board, 137; Roman Catholic Separate, 71; St. Catharines Board of Education, 52, 117, 132; Ukrainian Catholic Separate, 131
Schools. *See also Colleges & Universities, Day Care Centre*; PRIVATE; Magdalen College, 15; Phillips Private School, 122; Ridley College, 18, 85, 92, 120; Secondary; Grantham Academy, 14, 118, 119, 122; PUBLIC; ELEMENTARY; Alexandra, 128; Briardale, 132; Central (Merritton), 134; Central (StC), 123, 124; Connaught, 129; Court Street, 125; Edith Cavell, 130; Glen Merritt, 134; Glenridge, 131; Lady Spencer Churchill, 132; Main Street Schoolhouse, Pt. Dalhousie, 22; McArthur, 135; Memorial, 117, 123, 124, 130; North Ward, 133; Oakridge, 132; Port Dalhousie, 22; Queen Elizabeth, 131; Robertson, 124; Sir Winston Churchill, 132; Smythe Street, 133; St. Andrew's Ward, 123, 124; St. George's Ward, 124, 125; St. Patrick's Ward, 128; St. Paul's Ward, 123; St. Thomas' Ward, 123; Ten Mile Creek, 14; Valley Wood, 133; Victoria, 126, 127, 128; W.J. Robertson, 118; SECONDARY; Kernahan Park, 52; Sir Winston Churchill, 132; St. Catharines Collegiate, 118, 119, 122, 132; SEPARATE; Denis Morris High School, 136; École Immaculée-Conception, 124; Sisters of St. Joseph's Academy, 136; St. Bridget's, 82; St. Nicholas, 124; Ukrainian Catholic, 131
Sciamanda, Joseph, 73
Scott, Frank, 111; Henry, 111
Seiler, Hermann & Inge, 58
Seymour, Murton, 29, 54, 150
Shaver, C.G., Dr., 151
Sheahan, John, Dr., 151
Shickluna, Louis, 41
Shipbuilders: Muir Bros., 30, 36; Port Dalhousie Shipyards, 30; Port Weller Dry Docks, 30, 36; Shickluna, 32; Shickluna, Louis, 41
Ships: AUGUSTA, 111; DALHOUSIE CITY, 36; ONTARIO NO. 2, 36; WINDSOLITE, 36
Smith, George, Postmaster, 114; John, 7
Smyth, Ida, Miss, 133
Social Services: Children's Shelter, 37; Home for the Blind, 37; Lincoln County Industrial Home, 53; Merritton Senior Citizens Centre, 137; Merritton Senior Citizens' Centre, 147; Protestant Orphans' Home, 130, 154; Province of Ontario Early Childhood, 37; Queenchester Terrace Retirement Residence, 37; Red Cross, 137; Region Niagara Community Services, 83; United Way, 61; Women's Place, 127
Sparkes, Mary E., 58
Spencer, L.B., 75
Sports & Recreation: BINGO, Delta, 123; BOWLING; Dorado Lanes, 77; St. Catharines Lawn Bowling Club, 43; GOLF; Golf Club, Alexandra, 92; Golf Club, St. Catharines, 92; HORSES & HORSE RACING; Garden City Raceway, 100; Greenwood Raceway, 100; Kiwanis Horse Show, 100; Mohawk Raceway, 100; Ontario Jockey Club, 100; St. Catharines Riding and Driving Club, 52; LACROSSE Club, Athletics, 43; ROWING; Henley Regatta, 1903, 32; Henley Rowing Course, 100; St. Catharines Rowing Club, 32; SWIMMING; Lion Dunc Schooley Pool, 107; Merritton Lions Club Memorial Swimming Pool, 107; YMCA, 70; YM-YWCA, 70
St. Joseph's Convent, 136, 154
St. Lawrence Seaway. *See also Welland Canals*; 155; Opening, 141; Seaway Authority, 31, 155
Stanton, James, 114
Stewart, Gordon, 44
Stinson, Francis, 66; Samuel, 66
Stocking, Jerry, 99
Street Railways. *See also Bus Service, Railways*; NS&T, 27, 28, 116; St. Catharines Street Railway, 27; Thorold-Merritton Line, 27

Streetcar Manufacturers: Crossen Car Mfg. Co., 27; Preston Car & Coach Co, 27
Streets: renamings, 56; St. Paul St., one-way traffic, 1954, 69; surveying grid, 84
Suhacev, Igor, 24
Sundback, Gideon, 94

Tacinelli, Astride, 46; Marjorie, 46
Tait, James D., 61
Taylor, Dick, 111; Taylor, James, 87
Telegraph. *See also Radio & Radio Broadcasting*; Montreal Telegraph Co., 76; Services, 25
Theatres: Granada, 78; Grand Opera House, 77; Hippodrome, 64; King George, 78; Park, 78
Thompson, Richard, 55; Stanley, 92
Thorold: Conlon, Thomas, 49; gas lighting, 97; Hayes-Dana Ltd., 102; NS&T, 27; Waterworks (Merritton), 107
Toronto: Casa Loma, 75; F.C. Burroughes Furniture Store, 69; Greenwood Raceway, 100; harbour, 49
Transportation. *See Automobiles, Aviation, Bus Service, Railways, Shipbuilding, Ships, St. Lawrence Seaway, Streetcar Manufacturers, Street Railways, Welland Canals*

United Empire Loyalist: May, William, 58
United States, 10
Upper Canada, 58; Anti-slavery legislation, 1793, 10

VanDusen, Ralph G., 132
Victoria, Queen, 149
Vine, Kenneth, 80
Voisard, Edward, 44

Walker: James Nichol & Lida, 43; John, 62; Robert, 43; William Jr., 62; William Wallace, 62; William Welstead, 96
Wallis, Ald., 54
Wardell: Charles E., 23; Elmer, 23; Isaac, 23; Solomon, 23
Wars. *See also Aviation, Military*; AMERICAN REVOLUTION, 58; Armenian Genocide, 154; NORTHWEST REBELLION, 1885, 140; WORLD WAR I, 119, 150, 151; Fourth Welland Canal Construction, suspended, 35; G.W.R. Station, German Telegraph Operator, 25; McKinnon's, war production, 89; Ridley Memorial Chapel, 18; WORLD WAR II, 129, 131, 150; British Commonwealth Air Training Plan (BCATP), 150; Foster Wheeler, 95; Wartime Emergency School, 131
Watson, Alexander, Pvt., 140; Watson, William G., 68
Waud, Godfrey, 46
Weather: Merritton Tornado, 1898, 21, 55, 105, 133, 144; New Year's Eve storm, 1948, 29
Welland: NS&T, 27
Welland Canals. *See also St. Lawrence Seaway Authority*; Canal Construction, Union Tavern, 108; Conlon, John J., worker, 48; Customs House, 31; FIRST CANAL, 137; Lock 1, 56; FOURTH CANAL; Conroy Mfg., equipment supplier, 88; Engineers, 35; Forestry & Maintenance Branch, 35; Grant, Alexander Joseph, Engineer-in-Charge, 35; Land Expropriation (Hack Farm), 33; Lock 1, 34, 36; Lock 3, 155; Locks 1-3, 30; Planning, 35; Weller, J.L., Engineer-in-Charge, 31, 35; Irish Catholics Contribution, 11; Power Supply, Lincoln Transformer Station, 32; SECOND CANAL, 21, 53, 97, 110; Construction, 49; Lock 1, 111; Lock 18, 110; Lock 3, 32; Lock 6, 110; Lock 8, 104; Lock 9, 103; THIRD CANAL, 15, 24, 30, 71, 97; Gate Yards, 32; Lock 1, 30, 36; Woodruff, Samuel D., Engineer & Sup't., 39; Welland Canal Co. office, 31, 58
Weller, J.L., 31, 35
Western Hill, G.W.R., 26
Widdicombe, Arthur A., 74; Donald W., 74
Wiley, Thomas H., 45, 73, 78, 89, 126, 127, 129, 144 ;Thomas R., 38, 102, 149
Williams, John, 96
Wills, E.B., 82
Willson, Thomas L., 103
Wilson, Ernie, 59; George, Dr., 14; J., 99
Wood, Richard, 114
Woodall, John, Jr., 30; Woodall, John, Sr., 30
Woodruff, Hamilton K., 39; Samuel D., 39, 105; Welland, 39
Wright, Rufus, 15

Yates Street Heritage District, 46, *see also Heritage Designations*;
YMCA, YM-YWCA, 70, *see also Sports & Recreation*